Rituals for Home and Parish

Healing and Celebrating Our Families

Jack Rathschmidt, O.F.M.Cap.
and Gaynell Bordes Cronin

PAULIST PRESS
New York • Mahwah, N.J.

Interior art by Dean Vavek

Book design by Saija Autrand, Faces Type & Design

Library of Congress Cataloging-in-Publication Data

Rathschmidt, John J.
 Rituals for home and parish / Jack Rathschmidt and Gaynell Bordes Cronin.
  p. cm.
 Includes bibliographical references.
 ISBN 0-8091-3650-3 (alk. paper)
 1. Family—Religious life. 2. Catholic Church—Customs and practices.
 I. Cronin, Gaynell Bordes. II. Title.
 BX2351.R37 1996
 249—dc20
                   96-6797
                   CIP

Published by Paulist Press
997 Macarthur Boulevard
Mahwah, New Jersey 07430

Printed and bound in the
United States of America

Contents

vii   Introduction

1   CHAPTER 1   *Role of Ritual in the Life of the Home Church*

7   CHAPTER 2   *Connecting Family and Parish Rituals*

13   CHAPTER 3   *Creating Sacred Space in Our Homes*

20   CHAPTER 4   *Elements of Ritual*

26   CHAPTER 5   *Process of Ritual*

39   CHAPTER 6   *Types of Ritual*

41   LIFE CYCLES

Morning Reflection   *43*
Baby Shower   *46*
Birth   *49*
Baptism   *51*
Engagement   *55*
Wedding Shower   *57*
First Wedding Anniversary   *59*
Welcome Home Birthday   *62*
Birthdays   *64*
Blessing a New Home or Apartment   *67*
A First Day of School and Birthday (Multicultural)   *70*
Welcoming a Child's New Friend   *72*
Breaking Bread Meals   *74*
Blessing Cup Meal   *77*
Young Man Entering Puberty   *79*
Young Woman Entering Puberty   *81*
Leaving on a Trip   *83*

Returning from a Trip   85
Menopause   87
Helping the Elderly Let Go   89

91   GRIEF AND LOSS

Miscarriage   93
Facing Failure   96
Divorce with Dignity   98
Forgiving   100
Ending of a Friendship   102
Praying for Someone Who Is Ill   104
Anniversary of a Death   107
Death of an Abusive Person   110
Admitting Addiction   112
Losing a Job   115
Addressing the Pain of Special Family Days   117

121   THROUGHOUT THE YEAR

Celebrating Seasons   123
Advent   126
Thanksgiving   129
Christmas   131
Ashes from Ashes   134
Easter   137
Pentecost   140

143   Bibliography

Acknowledgments

COLLABORATION IS HARD WORK: painful, trying, joyful and exciting all at once. Many years ago we committed ourselves to team ministry, conscious that as lay woman and priest we could say much about women and men, lay and clergy working together as partners for the good of all. Our book has survived editing, changing, refocusing and refining because of our passion for the home church and our belief that men and women need to work together if we are ever to become the sign of God's reign that Jesus intended.

None of this would have been possible without the help of many people, especially our own families. The Cronin, the Bordes, and the Rathschmidt families challenged us for decades to take responsibility for ourselves, build up the body of Christ and nourish all of creation. We are very grateful to them.

We are also thankful to Doug Fisher, our supportive and patient editor at Paulist Press. Without his steady encouragement and the help of Lucille O'Connor, who read our manuscript and made many valuable suggestions, we may have been tempted to give up this project. The parishioners of Holy Name of Jesus, St. Theresa's, and Holy Name of Mary, and the Capuchin Franciscan friars, who always encouraged us to write and speak together, also deserve our immense gratitude.

Finally, to the countless families and religious educators to whom and with whom we have spoken, an enormous thank you. When you heard us explore the powerful possibility of the home church, you not only supported our dreams but shared your own stories and rituals with us. Because of you we believe a spirit of mutuality among families, parishes and churches everywhere will continue to grow.

Introduction

FOR A LONG TIME, WE HAVE WONDERED why most families seem so reluctant to try ritual prayer in their homes. We know we live in a hurried society with little time to mourn or celebrate wondrous moments. We also realize that families are so busy these days that most fail to gather regularly for meals more than two or three times a week.

Friends suggested that perhaps our culture was partly to blame. Instant coffee, minute rice and air travel that transports us to new countries and cultures almost instantaneously have stolen transition time from us. Not so long ago travel to another country or continent took weeks, even months. Travel time offered us the opportunity to let go gently and prepare ourselves for a new place. Travel provided us with a period of healthy waiting that fostered reflection and quiet prayer. Today most of us find it burdensome even to wait in line in grocery stores.

We are a people who want the speed of microwave ovens and fax machines that make it possible not to wait for anything. In the United States today, so committed to productivity, we try to fill up "in between" time with video games and television, which diminishes our appreciation of family and community. Our fascination with efficiency and individual accomplishment, moreover, often causes us to deny suffering and death, and hide our weaknesses even from our closest friends.

In a world such as this, God and religious tradition are often reduced to magic potions to which we go not for companionship and understanding but for instant answers. No wonder people are reluctant to celebrate home rituals! Rituals take time and demand we pay attention to loss and suffering as gifts calling us to healthy interdependence as families and churches.

But there was one final piece of our puzzle that only began to emerge as we traveled around the United States giving workshops. With frightening regularity, we heard story after story of family life in disarray. Marriages falling apart and children with discipline problems were only the tip of the iceberg. Slowly we began to realize that very ordinary people have been functioning reasonably well for years despite carrying almost unbearable emotional burdens including physical and sexual abuse. As the facade of normality and denial slowly crumbled, we began to understand why many people fail to pray as families.

People who carry terrible and terrifying scars find it very painful to celebrate rituals. Their unresolved guilt leaves them too ashamed to gather and tell their faith stories. They see themselves as broken vessels unworthy of God's love or concern. Reflecting on these stories convinced us that unless we find ways to admit and accept the hurt and pain that almost every family bears, we cannot hope to rebuild our home faith community through family prayer and ritual.

Several weeks ago we were invited to the home of friends whose only daughter, son-in-law and new-born infant were soon to move to the west coast. About a dozen people were present. While everyone fussed over the baby, perhaps as a way to avoid the pain of the young couple's leaving, it was obvious to us that despite her baby's presence, the young woman was near tears.

From our experience, the occasion begged for a prayer that would help all name how they were feeling, call on our shared faith as a rock of security in transition, and send this young family away with a deepened sense of how much they were loved. When we gathered for dinner, however, we paused only for a formal toast and began eating. While the gesture was beautiful, it seemed to come and go before anyone had a chance to reflect on its significance. Soon we were all saying goodbye. A chance for friends and family to bond themselves more deeply to one another at a happy but difficult time was lost.

We could only look at one another. We felt badly for everyone, but especially for the young couple. Almost every day, in one setting or another, we celebrate rituals that help heal us. We yearned to offer that same opportunity to all our friends.

What if our friends had celebrated a simple ritual for the young couple with two candles? First, they would have lighted a candle to the past, praying in gratitude for everything the young couple had meant in their family's life. Then they would have lighted a candle to the future asking God to guide this young family during their transition to a new part of the country. Finally, all would pause to ask God to help everyone live the present moment fully. We felt sure that a ritual as modest as this one would have lent tenderness, affirmation and honesty to a bittersweet day.

When we suggest that people regularly celebrate rituals, we do not mean our so called "morning rituals" like showering, brushing one's teeth or having one's first cup of coffee. While we usually do these actions in a repetitive way, they are not rituals in a formal or religious sense. They are tasks we do ritualistically.

For our purposes rituals are the attempts we make to express, through sacred story and symbolic gesture(s), our most important religious and spiritual values. These gestures and stories, many of which are proclaimed over and over like breaking the bread of the eucharist, are usually celebrated in groups and join us to other people through our shared belief.[1] While the actions we perform each morning are repetitive, there is rarely any deeply symbolic value to them.

Rituals have great power when they help us remember the past, plan for the future and honestly live in the present. They also help those celebrating them to make peaceful transitions in life. In fact, the repetition of rituals often begins to effect the change itself.

If, for instance, we decide to plant a tree in honor of a family member who dies suddenly, the actual planting of the tree helps us symbolically let go. When we also include some soil from the person's grave to nourish the new tree, we take a further step in accepting the unexpected death of someone dear to us. If, moreover, we visit and water the tree regularly, our attention to its new life deepens our commitment to living fully while continuing to honor the person who has died.

Furthermore, when we celebrate these life-changing events with friends and family we experience a new sense of belonging, not just to them, but to all of creation, and get a glimpse of what a meaningful community of faith can really be. We sense that our collective efforts can help make possible real and renewed commitment to the God who has promised to be among us, especially when we gather (Mt 18:20). And we pause to appreciate how much richer a simple gesture can be than mere words.

Parents live this last value every time they hug their children. We wonder what children would feel about their parents if they only heard the words: "I love you," and never felt their parents' arms around them. Gestures and actions make words come alive.

Authentic religious rituals therefore:

1. Honor and embrace our religious **past** with all its mistakes, joys, accomplishments and failures.

---

[1]Gerald Arbuckle in *Refounding the Church* (Maryknoll: Orbis, 1993) offers a more formal definition of rituals. They are: "the stylized or repetitive, symbolic use of bodily movement and gesture within a social context, to express and articulate meaning."

2. Challenge participants to reimage the **future** and discover ways to incorporate the values of the group into planning for tomorrow.

3. Are rooted in, respond to and express the felt spiritual needs of the family or community gathering **now.**

This last point marks the place where most religious rituals fail. Too often, the ritual actions of our parishes and families seem cut off from the stories they try to tell.

Some time ago we were giving a workshop in the southeastern United States. Gaynell told a beautiful story about her father. He had arranged to transplant a large oak to their new home so that his family would not have to wait too long to enjoy its shade. Eventually he also gave acorns from the tree to each of his children to remind them that like the acorn they could become almost anything as long as they worked hard and supported one another.

After listening to her moving story we asked the participants how they would have felt had we given each of them an acorn as they entered the seminar room? Without Gaynell's story, the gift of an acorn would have had little meaning. After hearing it, everyone wanted an acorn!

This book of prayer and ritual hopes to help families and parishes see everyday events, like sending adult children to a new part of the country, as fertile ground for spiritual growth. After outlining the role of ritual in the life of the home church,[2] we will explore the process of ritual, name its elements and emphasize the importance of creating sacred space in our homes. Then we will offer several life cycle rituals, prayers for grief and loss, seasonal celebrations, and demonstrate how home and parish might mutually support one another through ritual.

Finally, we offer two cautions. Since family prayer and ritual is sometimes threatening and uncomfortable, we can be controlled by family members who appear distracted or embarrassed. Not everyone likes or wants to pray in a group. That is understandable. Be patient with family members who are reluctant to join. But do ask those who are uncomfortable to trust for a while and just be quiet. Let them experience new ways

---

[2]*The Documents of Vatican II,* "Lumen Gentium," #11. Vatican II refers to families as "domestic churches." But because the word domestic is often used in American English to mean servant, we will substitute the term home or household church in this book. Home church seems to capture better the meaning of domestic church intended by official church documents.

of praying and see what happens. Deep acceptance will only come with time. Tolerance is all right for the time being.

Secondly, because rituals sometimes invite participants to dig deeply into their untold stories, someone needs to assume leadership. Unless one person invites all to gather, reflect and pray, family members might be reluctant to participate. Parents usually can assume a leadership role as a family learns how to be at peace while praying. Pick a leader for your family prayer and empower that person to create, direct and lead the prayer. After a while, leadership at rituals can move easily among members of a family, but in the beginning one leader helps the rest to relax, enjoy and appreciate the power of family prayer and rituals.

▸ *How do you tell your most important personal and family faith stories?*
▸ *Do you find it difficult to pray as a family?*
▸ *How do you help make times of transition in your family peaceful?*
▸ *Do you have family rituals?*

CHAPTER 1

Role of Ritual in the Life of the Home Church

EVERY SUNDAY WHEN I WAS a young girl growing up in New Orleans we ate our noon meal at grandma's house. I was always eager to arrive early so I could see grandma's homemade noodles hanging on the clothes line to dry.

It seemed that everyone came to my grandma's house. And if you wanted to bring a friend or friends, grandma would say, "Sure, bring them along." There always seemed to be room for someone extra. Grandma delighted in welcoming new people into her life. Once, when I was very young, I brought my best friend. But when grandma seemed to pay more attention to her than me, I decided not to invite her again. It took time for me to realize that grandma's expansive love extended to everyone.

With grandma's homemade noodles, she always served chicken—actually, one chicken. I know because I checked with grandma after I grew up. Still, there was always enough to go around.

I guess as I think back, maybe food was not very important. All present seemed to have their fill. The heart of the meal was talking and listening. Most Sundays it was the same story. Aunt Rita Mae talked about the hedge in her yard that grew so quickly it needed pruning every week. And Uncle Johnny, a sports referee, would talk about some controversial call he had had to make. My dad was a pilot and mechanic. He would update everyone about the latest conversion he was making on the amphibious planes which serviced the oil wells sprouting up all over the Gulf of Mexico. Every little bit of additional speed meant saving the life of someone trapped on an oil rig during a hurricane. And we children, we too, told our stories.

I always sat next to my great-uncle Albert. When I became impatient with the length of time it took to eat, he would lean over, touch me on the shoulder and whisper: "Gaynell, we are French. The French eat slowly. They savor their food in a calm, relaxed atmosphere." I never understood how our meal was ever calm. And anyway, there were football games to be played in the side yard.

Dessert was grandma's 1-2-3-4 cake which was so popular during the war years—one egg, two cups of sugar, three cups of milk, four cups of flour. On special occasions, confectioners' sugar was sprinkled on top. With the 1-2-3-4 cake, grandma served café au lait, a small amount of thick black coffee with chicory and boiled milk. It didn't matter how old you were. Even the children were served coffee.

And then the blessing. We never prayed before a meal. I don't know why. But after we ate grandma would thank all of us for coming and sharing our stories. And then we children would run up to grandma, give her a big hug, and run to the side yard to play. And that's my memory of growing up in the deep south when every Sunday we went to grandma's house.

▶ *How do you see yourself bringing grandma's faith to your family and community?*
▶ *Did you have a "grandma's" to go to on Sundays?*
▶ *What was it like?*
▶ *Does your family take time to rest and relax with one another?*

Gaynell learned wisdom and had planted in her the seeds of everything she would need to know about church, healing rituals and the eucharist at grandma's. She **gathered** with her family, **listened** to everyone's story, **broke bread** and was **sent** back to her everyday life. When these four actions of becoming church are present in our own homes, we are home churches. No notion will be more important than the term "home church" in this book. In fact, a growing appreciation of this concept will help families begin to develop a very different everyday faith and spirituality.

The idea of home church, while new to many contemporary Christians, is really a very old concept. Our Jewish ancestors were a community of table fellowship.[1] It is not difficult for us to imagine Mary gathering her family for sabbath and lighting two candles in her home each Friday evening. As the sun set she would thank YHWH for protecting her family

---

[1]Bernard Lee and Michael Corvan, *Dangerous Memories* (Kansas City: Sheed and Ward, 1986), p. 23.

during the past week and ask God to watch over them the following week. Between the two candles she would invite her family to rest, pray with and enjoy one another. We need to find similar ways to appreciate and celebrate the call to be home churches in our age. If we commit ourselves to gather, listen, share meals and send one another in faith, we will have made a good start.

▶ *What memories do you have of enjoyable family meals?*
▶ *What makes them memorable?*
▶ *What can you do to repeat the experience on a regular basis?*

Most of us realize that gathering is fundamental to our family's emotional and spiritual health. We often hear friends speak about how much they miss gathering as families when they are traveling or circumstances make it impossible. Still, families in our culture rarely gather for meals, fun and prayer. Our days are so full of things to do and events to attend that we find ourselves eating alone or on the run with almost no opportunity for conversation much less prayer. And gathering is only the first of the steps we need to take to strengthen our family life.

If we do gather but fail to listen to one another, the gatherings themselves become fewer. All of us know how difficult it can be when one person dominates conversation or disturbs the home environment through excessive talking, drinking or negative behavior. Trying to pray or celebrate rituals in this kind of setting can be almost impossible. When one person demands to be the exclusive focus of the family's attention, all the others hesitate to participate for fear they will upset the acting-out person. Listening in an environment like this is anxious and defensive.

That is why it is so important for families to have ways to address inappropriate behavior. I can still remember a four year old child stopping everyone's conversation by pointing to her sleeping grandfather and saying: "Grandpa's drunk again." While embarrassing for all, that child provided the perfect setting for discussing grandpa's behavior. That no one chose to do so is evidence that we simply do not fully appreciate the importance of our home churches.

On the other hand, when families gather peacefully they encourage all those present to tell their stories. Helping to create an atmosphere of peace is among the first duties for all present.

When I was a young boy, my uncle Joe often did this for our family. I grew up in a one bedroom apartment that housed six people. My dad worked twelve hour days and my mother was often tired tending to all our needs.

Uncle Joe, simply by visiting us weekly, provided mom a welcome rest, offered her adult conversation, and entertained us with his stories and songs. We liked being home, talking about the day, eating together and playing games. When I entered the seminary, the single most difficult thing I had to do was say goodbye to my family and our nightly gatherings.

Meals were the setting for most of our home rituals. We always prayed before eating, and birthdays were filled with favorite foods, homemade cake, candles and simple presents. Sunday dinners were special. I can still smell the roast beef and apple pie that drew us all to the table about two o'clock. We prayed, talked, ate and rested in preparation for the week to come. Our Sunday afternoon meal was our sending into the new week.

Meals were also the time when mom or dad made corrections and reminded us not to take anything for granted. I smile when I think about my mother's reaction one evening when I asked her if I could borrow some money for ice cream. She asked me how I intended to repay the loan. I reminded her that Aunt Katie was coming tomorrow and always gave me a dime. My mother scolded me, sent me to bed and reminded me that Aunt Katie's dimes were gifts, not privileges, and should never be expected. Mom taught me an important lesson about gratitude.

▶ *Does your family gather regularly for meals?*
▶ *Describe a typical meal.*
▶ *Can you make meals more enjoyable and faith-filled?*
▶ *Is there time for the telling of stories in your home?*
▶ *Is gratitude a theme at family gatherings?*

A deeper appreciation of the importance of becoming "home churches" naturally leads to the creation of home rituals. While books of home rituals are already available, it is our conviction that too often they recreate rituals for home use that are better suited for parishes and dioceses. We need home rituals rooted in everyday family life.

Only when we as families began to pay attention to our own experiences and deeply felt needs[2] for healing will we begin to create rituals that reflect where we are and not where others think we ought to be. Rituals that help families heal and celebrate the everyday and seasonal events they actually experience will help connect religion to daily life.

---

[2]Identifying our felt needs is a critical first step in creating home rituals. We will speak much more completely about how to do this throughout the book and especially in Chapters 3 and 4.

▶ *Can you think of your family as a church?*

▶ *What can make your home a vital church?*

▶ *What gets in the way of making this possible?*

Too often families, and especially children, talk about going to church as "boring" because it is disconnected from everyday experience. Inasmuch as parishes can only hint at all the issues affecting family life in their weekly rituals, the Sunday eucharist can feel boring. In our parish, which is a vibrant place with a dynamic and committed pastor and staff, the focus is on the *parish*. This emphasis, while understandable, makes it almost impossible for them to "gather up" the everyday events and needs of individual families in a way that helps everyone.

That is why we need to create home rituals. Too many families look to the parish to supply all their "spiritual fuel" on Sundays, putting a terrible burden on parish staffs to have perfect liturgies and prepare extraordinary homilies week after week. On the other hand, when families understand and begin to appreciate their call to be church and not simply go to church, they will gather at home, share their ongoing faith stories, break bread in memory of Jesus and send one another into the world as good news.

▶ *What are you experiencing as family right now?*

▶ *Do you celebrate home rituals?*

▶ *Can you think of some you could begin to celebrate?*

▶ *If you do celebrate family rituals, which ones do you like best and why?*

From this perspective, church begins at home, is gathered up in parishes and dioceses, and is celebrated cross-culturally in mission. Jesus' words calling us to "love one another" as a sign of God's reign take on new meaning. Families know what it means to love one another in faith at home. Moreover, when families' faith celebrations begin at home, they no longer depend on parishes and institutions to fill all their spiritual and religious needs.

Rather, they create new and mutually supportive relationships with their parishes and local churches that preserve the integrity of both the family and the parish. Assisting families to understand and establish their identity and importance as home churches ought to be one of the first tasks of parishes. With the appropriate help, families will then naturally create and celebrate their newly emerging identity as churches through ritual.

When I was a young girl, grandma was the presider and celebrant. She did not need permission to gather her family, listen to their faith stories, break bread with them and send them home renewed in God's spirit. Like God, grandma was a companion to her family in their messiness, and she convinced them that God lived among them as home churches.

Neither do we need permission to become church. We already are church at home. Discovering new ways to celebrate this reality will offer us a taste of "home holiness" we have never before experienced.

▶ *Do you depend on your parish for all your spiritual needs?*
▶ *What can you do in your home to help meet your family's needs?*

CHAPTER **2**

Connecting Family and Parish Rituals

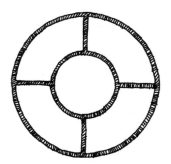

Sunday at grandma's was a gentle, refreshing and enlivening experience for me. Whenever circumstances made it impossible to be with grandma, I felt a real emptiness. More importantly, going to grandma's made me want to be like her. I have no question that Sunday dinner at grandma's was the most formative faith experience of my childhood. While I did not attend to it as a girl, Sunday afternoon at grandma's helped make sense of Sunday morning eucharist.

Home rituals, in our experience, far from substituting for parish celebrations, actually make Sunday eucharist more meaningful. In fact, we want to suggest even more. Not only will home prayer and rituals make Sunday eucharist more significant, but if we find the path to real mutuality between home and parish, both churches, home and parish, will benefit and grow. Mutuality between home and parish churches is the real key.

At the same time, we realize that the notion of mutuality between home and parish as churches is new and often accepted only in theory. Most parishes we visit, while honoring families as the foundation of their worshiping community, fail to seek them out as partners in religious and spiritual formation. That family prayer and ritual celebrated at home might have something to add to the spiritual life and religious formation of the parish is rarely acknowledged. That is why this book seeks first to help families learn how to create and celebrate authentic rituals at home. As families discover and develop their own religious traditions at home, they will slowly find their way into the life of the parish. Nevertheless, we continue to insist that mutuality as a value between home church and parish church is a realistic goal and should not be undervalued. A series of questions will help us appreciate mutuality more fully.

> ▸ *Do we as parents regularly seek to learn from one another as spouses?*
> ▸ *Do we ask about one another's needs and concerns or are we concerned exclusively with our children, finances, etc.?*

In our experience, roles for husband and wife, mother and dad, evolve slowly but clearly in most families. In itself we believe this is natural and necessary. But when roles become rigidly fixed in a particular pattern with little or no room for compromise, the marriage relationship slowly stagnates. Little if any learning goes on between the spouses.

In traditional family structures, for instance, the husband is the breadwinner and the wife is the homemaker. When, however, these roles determine decision-making in families, everyone loses. Husbands go to work each day, toil in a sometimes hostile environment, and return home to a family that has been interacting in many different ways throughout the day. If the husband is expected just to ask about everyone else's day, his work becomes devalued. It is merely the place where he goes to make the income everyone else needs to live.

On the other hand, if husband and wife take time regularly to ask about one another's day, its trials and joys, both spouses feel affirmed in their roles. When these kinds of conversations between husband and wife become an ordinary part of their lives, both parties feel important and loved in the other's eyes. They create a marriage relationship grounded in mutuality that allows and even encourages listening that leads to change.

In less traditional marriages, which are much more common, the value of mutuality becomes even more important. For many reasons women often choose to work outside their homes. If they are also expected to shop for food on the way home from work, cook the family meal and clean up afterward, resentment is sure to follow. On the other hand, when husbands, wives and children find ways to function well together to accomplish the everyday tasks of household living, everyone benefits.

Of course, by speaking about family and marriage we do not want to exclude single parents, the separated, divorced and remarried, or single people. Anyone who gathers with others in a regular way creates a kind of family with them. In fact, it may be even more important for people who often find themselves alone or ostracized from traditional gatherings to celebrate rituals regularly. Rituals can help us remember our joys while we pass through suffering. We are convinced that families of every kind who search for ways to honor and celebrate their uniqueness will grow in understanding and love.

▸ *How does your family structure affect your family prayer?*
▸ *What are the strengths and weaknesses of family life in your home?*

When families learn to respect each member and live well together, home prayer is natural and enjoyable. Moreover, families that pray at home find it easier to pray well in parish settings. Unfortunately, too many parishes still treat parishioners as passive recipients of liturgical actions and fail to capitalize on the rich experience of faith that people have on a daily basis in their home and communities. When this happens, pastoral ministers in parishes find themselves complaining about the lack of participation of their parishioners, and families have endless conversations about the inadequacy of parish liturgies.

We believe that when families are encouraged and helped to create rituals at home, they will naturally enter parish worship more easily and enthusiastically. The key to success is the mutual respect that must develop between families and parishes. When families learn to pray at home but find that their prayer has no place in the parish, they will tend to withdraw from parish life or join it in a minimal way. If parishes try to gather up the rituals and prayers of families for celebration in the parish it is possible that an entirely new atmosphere of sharing will grow.

▸ *Do you think your parish is interested in your faith life at home?*
▸ *If so, how does the parish show this?*
▸ *How would you like your parish to help you live a gospel life at home?*

We often ask a critical question when we do workshops about the home church: Does anyone from the parish or institutional church ask you how you decorate your home? Rarely does anyone answer affirmatively. In fact, most people look at us rather strangely. Their eyes ask: What does decorating our homes have to do with being church?

Our answer is: everything! For those of you who have been involved in renovating or redesigning your parish churches during the last twenty years, our point is very clear. Space is very important to people. Where we place the tabernacle, what kind of altar we choose, how we light our sacred space, what we do with memorial objects such as statues, windows and furniture—such topics generate an enormous amount of conversation and debate. And well they should. Each of our parish churches holds memories of baptisms, weddings, funerals, processions and popular devotions that shaped our everyday spirituality. When the space where we worship is changed, we feel as if we are being changed.

The same is true of our homes. Unfortunately, because the notion of home church is so new and we have yet to think of our homes as sacred places, we rarely reflect on the importance of decorating and arranging our homes. But if we accept the fact that our homes are churches, then we will be much more concerned with what they say about our values and faith.

Think, for instance, about the number of doors in most American homes. Are the doors passageways through which we enter and feel welcome or are they barriers reinforcing each person's privacy? Reflect also on the design of your kitchen. Is the person preparing the meal able to face everyone else and participate in conversation? Most importantly, we need to ask whether the lighting, the furnishings and the arrangement of each room in our home foster a spirit of hospitality and welcome.

Homes are churches. How we decorate and arrange them will help determine what we hope happens within our walls and what we want to say about our values to all who visit. We are not speaking about spending exorbitant amounts of money to do this. In fact, with a little creativity, a few well-placed lamps, the willingness to rearrange furniture and use nature, can make every home, no matter how simple, beautiful.

Moreover, until parishes take an active interest in the homes of the people who gather for worship on Sundays, a spirit of mutuality between home and parish will fail to materialize. After all, parish staffs hope their parishioners will take an interest in the design and beauty of the parish church. They must also find ways to show the same kind of interest in the design, adequacy and beauty of the homes of their parishioners.

▸ *How is your home decorated?*
▸ *Does it reflect important family values?*
▸ *If you could redesign your home, what would it look like?*

Many parishes have taken important steps in incorporating a family perspective in parish life. Some invite married couples to stand for election to the parish council and liturgy committees. Other parishes include the separated, divorced and remarried on their parish councils. Some, in order not to exclude those who are often forgotten, encourage single people to bring their understanding of family to parish meetings and gatherings.

But it is just as critical for the parish to take the next step. Parishes should invite families to reflect on the vitality of their homes as churches, and not just use them as resources to enhance parish life and worship.

A parish reflection group or continuing education program might encourage families to share the design of their homes with one another, not to criticize but to help all understand the profound impact our daily living space has on us. Newly married couples might also be invited to gather with one another and a few older couples to discuss how they have decorated their homes in order to make them places of welcome, hospitality, reflection and service. If there is no place to gather with a few friends, share stories and work together with others for the common good, it is very difficult to build a home church. When, however, families are encouraged to reflect on their uniqueness as churches, they are much more likely to appreciate and celebrate their relationship with their parish churches.

Growing up in New Orleans made Mardi Gras a very important day for me. Beginning on the feast of the Epiphany, we celebrated for months. When we moved to New York after our marriage, I was surprised how tame Shrove Tuesday was in the north. Soon after our oldest children were able to walk, we introduced them to a wonderful pre-Lenten celebration.

We dress in outrageous costumes, sing songs, parade around our home, eat delicacies like shrimp gumbo and oysters biennville, and bake a final King Cake. In New Orleans there are parties almost every week following the feast of the three kings. The person hosting the party puts a small plastic bean in the cake batter, then bakes it. Whoever gets the bean must host the next party. We baked our final King Cake and ate it in preparation for Lent.

Then, after the dishes from the evening meal are cleared, we gather around our kitchen table and place a strong metal bowl in the center. The bowl sits on a smooth stone. A small slip of paper is in front of each person. After all present have had a chance to speak about what they enjoyed most that evening, they take a moment to write a Lenten resolution on their paper and then place their folded paper into the metal bowl. The resolution can be anything. Some might write traditional forms of penance like fasting and extra prayer. Others might commit themselves to smile more, get involved in the community or take better care of themselves.

Then in silence one of the adults strikes a match and burns the paper in the bowl. After the paper cools, one person picks up the bowl, puts some ashes on his or her finger, and rubs the ashes on the forehead of the person to the right, saying: "I pray your Lent will be full of joy." Each person in turn anoints the person to the right with ashes.

The next day each family that has celebrated this ritual at home brings their ashes to the church where, at the first celebration of Ash Wednesday, they are mixed with the ashes of the other families and the parish ashes. Those marked with mixed ashes are reminded that they share in the hopes and resolutions of all the families of the parish.

This simple celebration clearly demonstrates the possibilities for rituals of mutuality between families and parishes. It really is wonderful to know as Lent begins that we never walk alone but with the commitment of other families who are trying to honor their call to be home churches. It does not take much imagination to dream about how other home rituals can be gathered up in our parishes, helping all the parishioners celebrate their interdependent faith. In fact, because we are convinced that both parishes and home churches will function better when they learn how to be mutually supportive, you will find numerous suggestions in this regard at the end of many rituals.

▸ *Does your parish foster a sense of mutuality between home and parish?*
▸ *What do you think are your family's responsibilities to the parish community and the parish's responsibility to your family?*
▸ *Can you think of any home rituals similar to the ritual of the ashes that can be gathered up and celebrated in parishes?*

CHAPTER 3

Creating Sacred Space in Our Homes

A MONG THE ELEMENTS NECESSARY for rich liturgical celebrations, none is more important than the space where we gather for prayer. When a church or a home is warm, softly lit, and obviously lived in, we feel welcome. Creating a hospitable environment is among the most important first steps that faces every group, especially our families.

There is a tree in my backyard—a fir, round and full. One side reaches for the morning light and shadows the herb garden. You can see her bottom trunk and roots pushing up from the ground.

One day, I removed the low branches for my granddaughter Sarah. I wanted her to know the evergreen as a canopy of protection from sun, rain, snow—a little shelter where she could sit still in nature and listen to her spirit: Sarah's spirit and the tree's spirit, too. We go there often. First we listen. Then we speak softly in story. This place has become a sacred space for us.

We had a difficult winter. Our evergreen was heavy laden with snow, ice, snow again. Finally winter's ice began to melt. I wondered how she could go through all the elements, battered and blown, and still be alive.

One early morning, sitting still in the kitchen, hot coffee in hand, I noticed how many birds the tree welcomed. Some were blue, others were red, brown, yellow and gray. They flew in, stayed a while, then moved on. Squirrels would dart in and out across the fallen needles which had formed a bed around the bottom—the same place where Sarah and I would always sit. Though I could not see into the fir's upper branches, I knew that there was space for all who came. Hospitality, graciousness, welcoming, like the mustard seed grown into the largest of bushes, were natural gifts of the evergreen. It seemed this place had become a sacred space for others, too.

Sacred space is the place where we meet others and tell our stories. It stirs our memories and becomes the occasion of hope. We might even call it "sacramental." Earthy and material, it is also transcendent because it is created and sustained by personal and communal meaning. Sacred place is ordinary place ritually set apart to be extraordinary. It becomes sacred because of the ritual acts performed there.

▸ *Where are your sacred places?*
▸ *What has made them sacred for you?*

Grandma's was a sacred place. We gathered there every Sunday. Her table soon became our family's storytelling space. Here we expressed our need to belong to one another and all creation through the ritual actions of gathering, storytelling, gesturing, and sending. Grandma always lit candles even though the sun streamed across the table from the southern windows. And there were fresh flowers. Always flowers. And iced tea in a dented, aging pewter pitcher. In the south a meal is not a meal without iced tea.

Sometimes there was a cloth on the table, but mostly I remember the worn oak wood-grain table with its support beam across the bottom where I put my feet. I can still smell the homemade noodles, some fried as a topping, the cake baking and coffee brewing. It was the same every week. I felt at home. I belonged. I was connected. I could dream and hope. I was comfortable. Even when the people invited each week were not family, they seemed comfortable, too. Our storytelling space was a safe place.

Because rituals help release and stir consciousness about basic feelings like longing and hope, joy and gratitude, loss and grief, sickness and pain, guilt and jealousy, wonder and surprise, we need an emotionally safe environment to explore and share them. Grandma's was always safe.

▸ *Where do you feel safe?*
▸ *With whom can you speak openly of your needs, dreams, hopes and pain?*

Because the environment at grandma's was safe, it was natural to celebrate intimate rituals there. We engaged our bodies, minds, senses, imaginations, emotions and memories. Because ritual encompasses the whole person, the senses are of particular importance. What we see, smell, taste, touch and hear can make us feel either welcome or guarded. More importantly, the associations we make through our senses about the place where we experience God linger long. Pouring tea from grandma's pewter pitcher, for instance, continues to awaken my memories and stir my faith.

History tells us similar stories about the importance of place. Augustine recalls exactly where he was in his garden at the time of his conversion. He also speaks of the children's voices calling to him to "take and read." And St. Francis returned all his life to the Portiuncula, the tiny abandoned church at the foot of Assisi's hills, to rekindle his vocation. Since their sensory feel never left the saints' memory, the garden and church became places to meet God.

▸ *Where do you experience holiness?*
▸ *Which one of your senses help you identify it in your memory?*
▸ *Is there a place where you go for nourishment and consolation?*

How we choose to decorate the rooms in our homes and arrange our furnishings also speaks boldly and clearly about what we believe. The objects, colors and plants express our values even more than our words. My childhood home was filled with plants, and the kitchen's curtainless windows opened wide as if inviting all of creation inside. The center of the table always had a sign of the season from nature. Flowers, stones, fir cones, pine needles and the containers that held them were earthy and simple. I often wonder how I ever noticed these objects. Except for meal times our table was always filled with the happenings of our day—newspapers, quilting, homework, notes and messages. The objects on our table told visitors much about our family values and concerns. No one minded setting the table for a meal but there were few volunteers to clean it beforehand.

Ortega y Gasset says: "Tell me the landscape in which you live and I will tell you who you are."

▸ *What is the landscape of your home and the rooms there?*

What do you suppose the rooms mentioned in scripture looked like? Remember when Jesus asked his friends to find a room appropriate for celebrating his final passover. One wonders what the environment was like and what Jesus' friends did to create a place of welcome and safety for Jesus and the apostles. We also read in the Acts of the Apostles that the apostles "went to the room where they gathered frequently to pray." What did this room look like? What objects were chosen to create an atmosphere for praying and storytelling? We have these same questions about Jesus' home in Nazareth. What did the home where Mary lit sabbath candles, passed the blessing cup and broke challah bread look like?

The medieval mystic Julian of Norwich asked similar questions in her quest to pray and enter more deeply into the mystery of God's presence. From her anchorage, her sacred space, Julian spoke of God as being courteous, familiar and homely. In order to imitate God, Julian created an environment friendly to mystery where she welcomed, listened, prayed and celebrated with all who came to visit her. Courtesy provided a safe place for storytelling which led to a deeper awareness of the sacred.

▸ *How familiar, homely and courteous is your sacred space?*
▸ *How friendly are they to mystery?*

As Julian's room, Sarah's evergreen tree and grandma's table offered a shelter to meet God, self and one another, so does the environment we create at home foster an awareness of the sacred and invite safe communion with the God who is already among us. In a home environment like this, transformation is made possible.

We need to create an environment which invites contemplation and sees beyond the face of the person or thing to sense the holy, the numinous, mystery.[1] If we want our homes to foster contemplation, we need to remember that something special can be experienced in everything that is seen, heard, touched, smelled and tasted.

In order to enhance the possibility for contemplation in our homes, the space we enter for ritual needs to be marked off, to have an area of focus, a point of orientation. It needs to be defined and circumscribed. Sitting in a circle, for instance, induces a sense of wholeness, unity and equality. Regardless of age or position, each person is important. Sitting in a circle also helps us foster a climate "of hospitality in which people are comfortable with one another; a space where people sit in view of one another."[2]

We also need to pay attention to what we place in the center of the circle since it will help us focus our attention. Tables, for instance, define space around which people can gather.

▸ *What memories do you have of your table growing up?*
▸ *What happened there? What memories does it stir?*
▸ *What happens around your home table today? What does it look like?*

---

[1] "Environment and Art in Catholic Worship," *The Liturgy Documents*, rev. ed. (Chicago: Liturgy Training Publications, 1985), pp. 269–99, #12. This document, while written to help parishes redesign their churches, is easily adapted for use in our homes.

[2] "Environment and Art," #11.

Like my grandma's table, these tables are sacred places because the people who gather there are holy.[3] Then we need to ask what we might place on our tables to mark special occasions or everyday events.

Recently, we asked second graders preparing for first eucharist to help set the altar table in church. In proud procession they brought the cloth and covered the wooden altar with candles, bread, wine, a bible and a picture of a special meal they remembered eating with their family. We talked about the meaning of each object on the altar.

Trying to make the connection between parish tables and home tables, we asked what was on their home tables for celebration. One little boy immediately began talking about tablecloths. He said there was a different colored one for each occasion. His family had a white tablecloth for "really special times"; a green one for St. Patrick's day—"we're Irish you know"; red for Christmas and "that day when you get a heart and candy"; orange for Thanksgiving—"a lot of fruit and turkeys on that one"; and black." Kevin's mother came to pick him up before we could find what occasion was marked with a black tablecloth!

The black cloth could certainly be a remembrance of the dead. In the Cronin home we mark the anniversary of someone in our family who has died by placing his or her picture on the table and lighting a memorial candle which burns throughout the day. On my dad's anniversary, there is also an acorn. The table is covered by a braided cloth, a sign of our lives being connected beyond death. On the anniversary of grandma's death we use a quilt she made as our ritual tablecloth. But perhaps like Kevin's family, a black cloth would be appropriate, too.

Kevin's sharing stirred my own memories of ritual cloths we use for our home table. We have colored tablecloths for the entrance into each season of the year and similar cloths for the different holy days and holidays. There is even a purple/green/gold one for Mardi Gras. Imagine those colors together! When our Mardi Gras cloth covers our table for the carnival season it reminds me of growing up in New Orleans.

▸ *What table coverings might you use to create an inviting environment for ritual at home?*

Kevin told me that when he walked into the house and saw the cloth on the table he "already knew what was going to happen before it happened because there was always something in the middle of the table." Even be-

---

[3]"Environment and Art," #65.

fore we speak, the environment invites, beckons and begins the movement toward celebration.

We also have signs on our table during the different seasons. In Lent, there are stones and a cactus plant on a purple swatch of cloth. In Advent, there are our family wreath and a small empty crib. Every day we see them and recall what happened there as we join in prayer and ritual together. It is an invitation to pause, to linger for a moment, and orientate oneself to what is happening in our family life. Walking into the kitchen or dining room, the environment speaks of what is happening.

Some families have colored banners for each season of the year. The banners both remind them of where each person is and invite them to get in touch with the God experienced in each season.

▸ *What seasonal decorations, signs and colors might you use to deepen your awareness of God?*
▸ *What could you place in the center of the table to remind everyone of a special day?*

We also have spaces in our home for personal rituals that help us express and remember our daily walk with God. Some people have a night table upon which they place important objects, flowers or candles. Others use a corner of their desk this way. Whenever I sit in a particular chair in my office, I assume the ritual act of silence. When we attend to our "altar" daily, we are symbolically recognizing the sacred within ourselves and the world.

Like Sarah's space under the fir tree, we also have outdoor spaces that we make sacred by gathering ritually in them to celebrate wedding anniversaries, engagements, baby showers, birthdays, and new school years. We also gather for events like Memorial Day, the Fourth of July and Labor Day. We assemble in our side yard and form a circle. Sometimes we have a sign in the center of our circle to help us focus on the day. In recent years, our oldest grandchild rings a small bell before each gathering. When everyone is present the other grandchildren join in the bell ringing. Then we usually hold hands and offer a word of recognition or thanksgiving. Simple but profound, these ritual prayers remind us of who we are and who we hope to become.

We speak of space as having a "good feeling" when it is a place of hospitality and graciousness.[4] We call the environment appropriate when it is beautiful and in need of a group of people to complete it.[5] It also sug-

---

[4]"Environment and Art," #51.
[5]"Environment and Art," #24.

gests that furniture and other objects have a symbolic function second in importance only to the people who gather. Space profoundly affects our experience of self and God and often directs the actions of the people.

The following questions may facilitate creating a space for ritual in your homes. The answers will help your family identify when they are most aware of the sacred.

- ▸ *Where will you gather?*
- ▸ *What will make you physically comfortable?*
- ▸ *What will offer all emotional safety?*
- ▸ *How will you define the space?*
- ▸ *What will be your area of focus?*
- ▸ *How will you sit or stand?*
- ▸ *What decorations are appropriate?*
- ▸ *What furnishings do you need and how will you arrange them?*
- ▸ *What kind of lighting will enhance the space?*
- ▸ *How will the environment engage the senses—sight, smell, touch, hearing, taste?*

Before a word is uttered, the environment welcomes and accepts you and sets the theme for the ritual.

Our home space is sacred. We make it even more so when we gather there regularly to share our lives, faith and rituals that help us express without words all our hopes and dreams.

CHAPTER 4

Elements of Ritual

PERHAPS YOU HAVE GIVEN A PLANT to friends celebrating the birth of a child. No doubt your gift was an attempt to say without words how happy you were for them. In offering people gifts or objects that may have value in themselves, we are also telling them symbolically how much we care for them and that we hope they will make transitions in their lives gracefully and peacefully. While most people use the elements (air, water, fire and earth) and senses (hearing, smelling, seeing, tasting and touching) as foundations for their celebrations, the only limitation is our imagination.

Symbolic gifts have both a level of universal and personal meaning.

Personal Symbols

I cherish my toe shoes and cannot throw them away. When I was young, ballet was my great passion. Even today, when I pick up my toe shoes I can still hear the music I danced to long ago from "The Flight of the Bumble Bee." I had been so frightened to go out on that stage all alone. Would I remember the movements? I had practiced long hours but now it seemed the choreographer was asking me to do the impossible. I wanted to run away. What if I made a fool of myself and everyone laughed?

These fears released other insecurities. Then, from the depths of my memory, I heard the words my mother always spoke whenever her children faced a challenge: "Just try." Somehow I moved out on stage. The music began. Within seconds I was caught up in the beauty of the movement. I can still hear the clapping and approval of the audience. My toe shoes are a symbol of personal meaning to me and represent a turning point in my life when I let go and trusted in God and my training.

Personal symbols as seemingly insignificant as my toe shoes can transform us. Teilhard de Chardin says it this way: "Three things, tiny and fugitive—a glance, a song, a sunbeam. I thought they had entered me there to remain forever. Instead, they embraced me and bore me away." While tiny and fugitive things happen unexpectedly to Teilhard, in ritual we choose our symbols and are surprised by their ability to transform us.

Symbols point beyond themselves with a power greater than themselves. In ritual, symbols are the vehicles one takes to connect with others, creation, and God. They are the language of the soul. Symbols in ritual move and instruct us; they put us in touch with meaning and mystery in a way nothing else can.

After my grandmother died, my aunt gave me the wooden spoon she had always used to make her 1-2-3-4 cake. I treasure that spoon because it not only reminds me of grandma but it also resurrects the feelings associated with going to her house. The shawl she knitted me does the same thing. How can I forget her telling me that with every stitch she thought of and loved me. My toe shoes, my grandmother's wooden spoon, a shawl are all symbols of deep personal meaning to me.

▶ *Has anyone given you a gift that has become a symbol for you?*
▶ *How can we speak symbolically to one another as family?*

Universal Symbols

Families, groups, nations and churches have symbols, too. Jack speaks of the one hundred year old christening gown worn at every baptism in his family. It roots his family in the past, binds them together, and invites all to renew family relationships. For many Americans, the flag is a symbol which honors personal freedom, independence and the pursuit of happiness. The church speaks of universal symbols all the time, not the least of which is the breaking of the bread at eucharist.

▶ *What symbol speaks of who you are as family right now?*
▶ *Do you highlight and celebrate your family life through symbols?*

Almost everything in nature can have symbolic value. Using water to wash our face or hands can be a symbolic cleansing after an unpleasant experience. Putting on new clothes can be a symbolic renewal. Disposing of old things reminds us to "let go." Burning paper on which we write our fears not only releases us from the fears, but the smoke, like the ancient burnt offerings, becomes a symbolic link between God and us.

The symbols we choose indicate the transformation for which we yearn. Invoking the symbol helps bring about that transformation. Weeding our gardens, for instance, clears out all that impedes growth, not only in the garden but within us as well.

The symbolic gesture of drawing, cutting and disposing became a symbolic release for a six year old girl. Courtney was diagnosed with cancer when she was four. Two years later, after many treatments, she was in remission, a healthy and active child. At the same time, her grandmother became ill with cancer and went to the hospital. Courtney and her mother visited. Everyone remarked on the tender compassion Courtney had for her grandmother.

But during the grandmother's hospital stay, Courtney's behavior in school and around the house began to change. She became depressed and despondent. Although her mother sat and talked with her, she feared her cancer had returned. Her mother asked Courtney to draw a picture of herself pinpointing where the cancer was in her body. Then she gave Courtney a pair of scissors and asked her to cut out the cancer. Courtney then placed the cut-out in the trash can and tightened the lid on top. Her mother assured her the cancer would not return.

Choosing an appropriate symbol usually flows from the story we are telling. After clarifying our intention, we ask ourselves what symbolic elements will help us tell our story through gesture. Intuition and an inner voice help determine what symbol will affirm us and bring about change. As our awareness of the symbols we use deepens, we more fully experience a sense of sacredness in ritual.

A few years ago a young friend experienced a painful divorce. Although there were no children in his marriage, "Bill" felt like a terrible failure. He was especially dreading the celebration of Christmas that had become such a central part of his family's life. Although he knew he had to be with his family, he wished he could skip Christmas that year and make believe his marriage never happened.

Bill once told me: the hardest place to be is no place! All of us have resided in those uncomfortable places of transition—between jobs, relationships and even marriages. We have felt uprooted, disconnected and marginalized. We are not sure where or to whom we belong. At times such as these, family celebrations can be painful.

Like so many others who are in transition, "Bill" needed a ritual to express his ambivalent feelings. Because he was a deeply religious person, I suggested he make Advent a time of healing for himself. I asked him to take time each day after work to visit his parish church. On entering the church, he was to take water from the font and bless himself in union with everyone who experienced divorce that year. After a few minutes of trying to be present to the recently divorced, he was to light a candle for another divorced person. Late in the afternoon on Christmas eve he found himself in church. As he approached the candles before the tabernacle, he began to think of and then pray for his former wife. With many tears, he lit a candle for her and felt a wave of relief flood his body. He knew the process of healing had begun. He was ready to be with his family again on Christmas.

▸ *Do you have a personal story that could benefit from a prayer ritual?*
▸ *Do you carry anger and hurt that needs healing?*

Life's transitions can be difficult. During the change of seasons, many cultures sprinkle water on their homes and crops, hoping with this symbolic gesture that the gods will bless their dwelling places and fields. Still others bury food with their dead to help the departed on the rest of their journey. No matter what gesture or symbol we choose, the human family senses its need to express ritually its recognition of the bittersweet nature of change.

Every week eight women friends gather in a circle in my home around a coffee table. The tablecloth comes from Bolivia. On it sits a circle of small warming candles enclosing a center sculpture of three people in movement. Instrumental music plays in the background and a small stick of burning incense welcomes all.

After we gather, each person takes a few moments to image the rising incense cleansing a space in the room. Then, inhaling the smoke, all imagine their breath cleansing a space within them for listening. Each woman lights a candle and while doing so names a particular need. Then in the sacred circle we have created with our lives, we share on the theme we have previously chosen. This is our sacred space, and the actions and stories we share stir memories, heal wounds and offer hope.

The actions as I have described them are orderly and repetitive. Once when I tried to change the order because I had failed to buy incense and warming candles, people were noticeably upset. Another time they protested because I used *our* music to settle a larger group of people gathering on Christmas eve. My women friends told me *our* music sounded strange in another environment. Somehow the pattern of calming the mind and inviting the senses to rest as a way of centering ourselves belonged to us around our coffee table. Ordinary space had become sacred because of the ritual actions we had celebrated there.

Imagination is our only real limitation in creating rituals for our homes. The most common elements can be used to express in sacred gesture what cannot be expressed adequately in words. Our intention, however, is not to limit your creativity but to help you get started. The more you practice creating rituals, the more your own faith and family life situations will direct your efforts.

▸ *What do the following elements say to you?*
▸ *Which one would symbolically express your family's life right now?*

  ▸ **Fire** (flame, candle, fireplace, match, sparklers)
    Is your family warm, inviting, passionate?
    Are there resentments smoldering in your family?
    Do you need light for direction or to see in the darkness?
  ▸ **Water** (waves, fountains, rain, river, streams)
    Is your family in need of refreshment, cleansing, cooling?
    Are you thirsty for growth and change?
  ▸ **Air** (scents, kites, flags, wind, feathers, sounds, bells, wind chimes, drums, gongs, windsocks)
    Does your family life feel stifling, in need of fresh air?
    Do you want to send your family's strengths to others?
  ▸ **Earth** (stones, seashells, baskets, wreaths, rocks, flowers, petals, wood, branches, trees, acorns, soil)
    Do you enjoy your family's earthiness and concern for the environment?
    Do you need to bury old hurts?
    What and who are the rocks in your life?
  ▸ **Food** (seeds, breads, fruits, beverage, herbs, spices, salt, oil, sweets)
    Are meals important to your family?
    Do you feed one another with your sacred stories?
    What kind of nourishment and strength do you need in life?
  ▸ **Clothing** (shawls, coats, capes, silk, burlap, tablecloths)
    Is your family a warm, safe place to be?
    Do you clothe one another with compassion and love?

▶ *What do the following gestures say to you? Could any of them symbolically express what is happening inside you right now or what your family is experiencing?*

▶ Digging	▶ Planting	▶ Eating	▶ Harvesting	▶ Silence
▶ Rubbing	▶ Sprinkling	▶ Pouring	▶ Washing	▶ Hugging
▶ Clapping	▶ Kissing	▶ Blessing	▶ Braiding	▶ Mingling
▶ Swaying	▶ Dancing	▶ Singing	▶ Chanting	▶ Bowing
▶ Walking	▶ Kneeling	▶ Giving	▶ Receiving	▶ Turning
▶ Ringing	▶ Coming/Going			

CHAPTER 5

Process of Ritual

Ritual Format

FAMILIES AND PARISHES CAN CREATE effective and beautiful rituals in their homes and churches. We use the circular pattern sketched below to help people create rituals which celebrate who they are and hope to become. Begin in the middle of the circle and proceed clockwise.

INTENTION   Ask yourself the question: What are our family's needs? What must we recognize, honor, support and heal? How shall we begin? We call this identifying the FELT NEED of the family or group. Clarity and honesty about this first step will allow families and groups to identify their intention(s) and move easily through the four action steps of the ritual.

GATHERING | Having identified our intention(s), we ask ourselves the question: With whom should we gather to pray about and celebrate the felt need identified—e.g. grandparents, friends, schoolmates?

STORYTELLING | In light of the felt needs of those gathered, what personal, family and scripture stories come to mind to help us name and pray about what we have already identified?

GESTURING | Gestures or ritual actions allow all to participate without words. What gesture helps us express our felt needs without words—e.g. lighting candles, joining hands, bowing? Consult the list at the end of Chapter 4.

SENDING | A simple prayer, blessing, song or gesture helps send us back to our everyday lives renewed after honestly naming our felt needs and finding ways to express them through gesture and story—e.g. extending hands in blessing, hugging goodbye.

REFLECTION | *(Optional)* Though not always possible, our experience tells us that people want and need to talk about what they experience at prayer and ritual. A few minutes for reflection offer all an opportunity to share what happened to them, what they learned and how they might want to live the gifts they gained around their home tables.

To foster reflection at the end of rituals you might ask: What question(s) might help reinforce the power of the ritual we have just celebrated? What question(s) might help our family experience the joy of family living? Did the ritual offer us new insights about our family? Are we moving toward transformation because of the feelings that stirred in us during the ritual?

As ritual makers, let us take a closer look at each of these movements.

Intention

Paying attention to our felt needs as individuals and communities is the key to authentic and meaningful ritual celebrations. Felt needs help us isolate the intention for prayer and ritual and remind us to what we must pay most attention. Gaynell learned about felt needs at grandma's.

Grandma knew how important it was to gather as family. That is why she created a safe environment for her children and grandchildren to gather every Sunday. While she hoped that her home would provide a haven where honest conversation flourished, she was even more interested in the simple fact that her family was together. Her intention was clear. She wanted her children and grandchildren to be together regularly. She was convinced that too many families drift apart because they get out of the habit of gathering. For grandma, getting together was fun, enriching and empowering. When her family came together, especially in difficult times, good things happened.

What are your family's felt needs? Is someone sick? Is someone leaving for college? Is your family in sharp disagreement about education, religion or politics? The answers to each of these questions tells you your family's intention.

Recently, my husband Jim was diagnosed with cataracts. Although he knew that cataract surgery had become routine, he was anxious. His eyes were everything to him. His favorite form of recreation and relaxation is reading. He needed to talk about his apprehensions and his family needed to find a way to respond to his needs.

On the Sunday evening before Jim's surgery, everyone gathered for supper. Before the meal all took a few moments to think about something they really enjoy seeing, after which Jim spoke of the people and things he most enjoys seeing. Everyone then extended their hands toward Jim and together blessed his eye with the hope that he would be able to enjoy the things he mentioned even more after his surgery. It was a gentle moment that candidly named our fears and hopes and allowed us to reach out to Jim with prayer and tenderness.

▸ *How would you reach out to someone's fears in your family?*
▸ *How would you like others to reach out for you?*

Birthdays, graduations, baptisms, weddings, engagements and so many events are natural times for celebrations. When we are able to say clearly what we want to happen at times like this, we will be able to create rituals that respond authentically to our family's actual felt needs. The more honestly we listen to our innermost needs, the more we will be able to create prayers and rituals that touch, move and help us change. Identifying our felt needs is the first and most fundamental step in crafting creative rituals for our families.

Gathering

When I was a boy, supper was at 5:30 every weekday evening. There were no adequate excuses for not being on time for supper. My mother liked her food hot and all four kids were expected to be around our small kitchen table with hands washed, ready to pray when mom passed our plates to us. For those of us who grew up in cities, a mother's cry from the third floor window of an apartment building still echoes in our memories. It really didn't matter whether there were two outs in the ninth inning of our stickball game. When your name was shouted, you left whatever you were doing and ran for home. Meals were important events at which we felt the power of family and learned to pray simply. While food was rarely fancy, the regularity of meals together lent a special rhythm to our family life and planted the seeds of an everyday spirituality whose power continues to shape our lives today.

For centuries, Catholic Christians focused on the priest presider and the words of institution when naming what is most important when we go to mass. However, when the liturgy committee of the U.S. Bishops' Conference wrote: "Among the symbols with which the liturgy deals, none is more important than the assembly of believers,"[1] they challenged parishes, dioceses and families to shift their focus and remember that Jesus is present among us not only when the priest leads us in the eucharist prayer but whenever we gather in his name.

When we fail to appreciate the God who lives among us when we gather, too often the eucharist becomes a personal devotion fostering individual holiness. On the other hand, when we ground ourselves in the wonder of God's life as we gather, the eucharist becomes a time to gather up everything that happens in our daily lives.

The phrase "Nothing is more important than the assembly of believers" is critical for families and households to hear again and again. When we fail to appreciate the significance of gathering at home to listen to one another, tell our everyday faith stories and break bread, we cheat ourselves of developing an authentic eucharistic spirituality of the home.

▸ *Do you believe that Jesus lives among you when you gather as family?*

▸ *What is a good way to reinforce this belief?*

---

[1] "Environment and Art," #28.

Gathering as families, especially for meals, is becoming an increasingly infrequent event in the United States. The proliferation of fast food restaurants and microwave ovens bears testimony to this fact. Our families are so busy that we rarely have time to sit together, share a meal and catch up with one another's lives.

Without being naive about the demands of family life as we move into the twenty-first century, we still believe that gathering regularly as a family is fundamentally important for our collective well-being. This is even more true for stepfamilies and blended families. Our culture, imaging life like a raging river, urges us to jump in and hope we're still alive when everything calms down. When we do come to a quieter place, we are often too tired from the trip to pay attention to one more thing or one more person. Nevertheless, in our experience, when families make time for one another especially at mealtime, they almost always find a strength they simply cannot develop alone.

Gathering is the first step in building our faith families. Try to pause for a few moments of quiet when you are able to gather as families. Even a few seconds of gentle, rhythmic breathing will help us appreciate that when our families gather we are more than the sum of its parts. We belong to one another and to all families. We belong to the world and all creation.

The place where we gather, no matter how humble, is holy.

Take a moment to appreciate the wonder of God's presence among us when we gather. Rejoice in the awesomeness of who we are becoming when we share faith stories. Celebrate our power by breaking bread together. And remember: "Nothing is more important than the assembly."

Since gathering is the first action step of any ritual, the leader needs to help the group focus and recognize its sacredness. Lighting a candle, ringing a bell or initiating a breathing exercise helps alert everyone that the ritual is beginning. In our experience, home rituals work best when there is a clear and invitational beginning.

Storytelling

I was almost forty years old and a priest for many years before I heard my parents' faith stories. One especially helped me understand a dimension of my family life that had never made sense.

One Christmas when my parents were visiting me at our college seminary where I was teaching, they told me about my older brother Joseph. Named after my dad, he was a healthy, vibrant child. Shortly after Christmas in 1939 my parents hosted a party for their friends in our apartment building. My eldest sister Ronnie and brother Joseph were put to bed early. Mom checked on them midway through the party. They were both fine. When their guests left shortly after midnight, mom and dad were both tired. My mother still regrets that she and dad simply went to bed after everyone left without checking the children a second time. The next morning after dad left for work, my mother went to check on Joseph. He was cold, already dead for several hours. Near hysteria, she called the fire department which responded immediately with emergency equipment. The oxygen mask they put over Joseph's face did no good. In the meantime, the police went to my father's office in New York City and told him there had been an accident and to return home as soon as possible.

My mother, crying still after almost forty years, was ashamed to admit that she was more afraid of my father's possible judgment of her as a negligent mother than she was of facing Joseph's death. When dad finally got home after almost two hours on subways and buses, there were no harsh words of recrimination. They simply held one another and cried. The next day dad was incensed because a headline in the local newspaper suggested a too large nipple on Joseph's bottle may have caused his death. In the 1940s no one had heard of Sudden Infant Death Syndrome. Citing the coroner's report that the baby's death was from unknown causes, my father wrote to the newspaper demanding they retract the story and restore mom's good name. Dad's gestures of support for my mother were the ground upon which they built the rest of their marriage.

By the time my parents finished telling me their story, we were all crying. For the first time in my adult life, I realized why my mother was often overly protective of her children. I also understood why she was so anxious when her grandchildren were born. The pain she and dad had felt was so powerful that she did not want her children to experience it. Even after more than forty years of grieving there was a part of them that still needed to tell their story in order that healing could continue.

▸ *Recall a faith story from your family?*
▸ *How does it affect your family today?*
▸ *How can we help one another tell our family faith stories?*

Of course, devastating events like the death of an infant do not visit every family. But other areas in need of healing surely do. What family has not experienced addiction to drugs, alcohol, food, work and so much more? Unless we attend to these compulsive problems that radically alter our family's lives, we can never be healed. People in twelve step groups like Alcoholics Anonymous and Al-Anon tell us that we are only as sick as our secrets. They also remind us that when one person in a family picks up a drink, drug or food unhealthily, six people get sick.

What if I had never heard my family's tragic story of marriage, faithfulness and strength? I would have been cheated of a part of my history that was vitally important to my developing a faith perspective. My parents' faith story immensely increased my respect and love for them as well as my gratitude for my faith.

Families need to tell one another their personal faith stories. While this is usually done around the kitchen table, it can happen in bedrooms before sleeping and in cars on trips. That our stories are told is most important. Without them our faith is often a heady commitment to an unknown God who controls us out of fear. With them our faith life becomes rooted in the heart of our everyday experience and colors and shapes everything we do and become.

Telling our family faith stories also helps us choose the ritual gesture(s) that follow. For Gaynell, at her grandma's house everyone was mentioned by name and hugged at the end of the meal. These gestures emerged directly from the stories grandma heard.

When my aunt Rita Mae spoke of her husband's illness rather than the side hedge, grandma spoke her name and hugged her. When my dad admitted that a project he was working on failed, grandma hugged him. Calling her children's names and hugging them told them they were not alone. Grandma's gesture spoke powerfully of her acceptance of all her children, no matter how difficult their life might be. Grandma loved them just as God did.

Several years ago Jack was asked to help bury a young man who had committed suicide. After spending time with the family, and listening to their loving stories of the young man's life, he celebrated the boy's funeral. Afterward, because the young man had been cremated (in accordance with a decision made by the entire family concerning their respective funerals), they asked Jack to help them with a personal ritual.

The young man loved fishing, especially the streams and small rivers near his home. A few weeks after his funeral, his family took his ashes to the young man's favorite stream and sprinkled them in the fast moving current. As they prayed for the courage to let go of him they also prayed for themselves. Their eloquent gesture helped everyone begin the process of healing.

And what if we never hear the scriptures, our faith stories? Just as the commitment of Jack's parents to one another and to God were deepened because of their faith, so too is our faith strengthened when we remember biblical stories and lessons. That is why we suggest that every family ritual have a place for scripture as well as our personal stories. Seeing how our faith experience is a continuation of the faith of believers who have walked before us can help all grow in the realization that God's Spirit is still with us. Scripture is a living, breathing collection of stories whose intent is not simply to inform us about God and Jesus but to let us hear how people experienced God's love in their lives.

To be a family is to have a story. Stories tell of the zigzags in our lives. They chart the struggles, transitions and transformations. When told with honesty and not sparing the pain and hurt sometimes buried deep inside, they can even heal our memories. When we tell our family stories, we sense we are related to a large mystery. We reclaim our heritage and remember that we belong to one another.

Family stories are religious tales very much like scripture. Scripture is the community's attempt to remember its experience of God as a compassionate and loving presence. Choosing and telling scripture stories in family ritual reminds us that we are God's ongoing story. When we proclaim the stories of yearning, pain, joy and gratitude embedded in God's word, we remember similar family stories. Often when we recount family stories, a scripture story will come readily to mind. The scriptures we offer are merely suggestions intended to stir your memories. Whenever possible, choose a scripture story that seems most appropriate. Sometimes you may want to comment on them. At other times, you may choose to read, remain silent and allow the scriptural images to stir the listeners' hearts.

Tell your family faith stories. Tell them over and over. And read the scriptures to one another regularly. Good stories never get old.

Gesturing

Rituals have always been important to me. I first learned of their value at grandma's. While I rarely see noodles hanging on clotheslines, clothes hung out to dry in a brisk spring breeze remind me of grandma's house on Sunday afternoons. Grandma also taught me the importance of personalizing prayer. Grandma had the ability to remember what she had heard that day and never failed to ask God to respond to the needs of her children and grandchildren before sending us off for another week.

But gestures speak even more loudly than words. I always knew grandma loved me. She made me feel important by inviting me to help in meal preparation, knitting me shawls and calling me every time she saw my name in the paper for the most insignificant events.

Think of the gestures we use to speak to our spouse, children, and friends. When was the last time you sent a card or gift to say "I love you" without words?

My dad also taught me much about the importance of gestures. He was one of the quietest men I ever knew, yet when he wanted to say something important, he spoke eloquently through gestures. I will never forget the full grown tree he had transplanted to our new home so we would have some shade from the intense summer sun of New Orleans.

I also remember the first time I had a car accident. Upset, I called him, told him what was wrong and waited for his response. He assured me I had done everything correctly, asked me if I could drive the car, and told me to come home after I finished my errands. His gentle tone filled me with the confidence I needed to accept the accident for what it was: a minor scratch that would be easily fixed and not a cause to review my entire life. My dad's ability to respond without anger or fear began my healing. Without his sensitive response, I surely would have worried needlessly about an event that really was accidental.

Gestures remain deeply important in my family life. Each Sunday when our family gathers for the evening meal, we light two candles. We light the first in gratitude for the past week and the second in the hope that the week to come will be safe and faith-filled. Then we rest between the light of both candles, hold hands and pray from our hearts about our needs, fears and wants.

We also often hang simple banners of purple, green, white or red to remind us of both the liturgical seasons and nature. Our banners remind each family member to treasure the seasons of the year and invite us to enter more deeply into the spirit of each special time. Passing the blessing cup regularly also helps us listen better to one another's dreams, fears and joys, while breaking bread when we sit down for a meal challenges us never to forget those without food.

By borrowing a custom from our Indian brothers and sisters, we have also found a way to heal one another of family hurts. The gesture is simple and profound. In silence all extend a hand gently toward the group, fingers together and upright. This greeting says: "May you have nothing to fear from me, nor I from you."

These gestures seem natural to our family. We want to thank God for being a light in our lives and ask God to continue to light our family's path.

We need to find ways to listen to the song of each season and we are anxious to create an atmosphere of peace in our family and world. The gestures we choose to help us honestly name our needs and celebrate our joys emerge from everyday living situations. The same, we feel sure, can be true in all our families.

Think about the symbols you use every day to express love, hurt, hope and friendship. They will tell you so much about your family spirituality. More importantly, they will help you discover ways to grow in God's love each day.

Sending

Claire, our oldest child, announced her impending wedding and her intention to do a year of service in Latin America within days of each other. Naturally, while we were overwhelmed with joy, delight, suspense and fear, we struggled to let her feel our deepest support and admiration. Clearly, Claire had gone off to college a girl and returned a woman. Though still quiet, she wanted to live an independent and interdependent life, and her joint announcement signaled that. We knew we needed to find a way to send her into marriage and the third world with faith and gladness.

Sending can be the most difficult part of ritual celebrations. That we are all called to mission through baptism is a simple truth of our faith. That we also want to hold on to our children, friendships and possessions is a fact of our human existence. After all, we argue, relationships are hard work. Why should we let them go?

Jesus offers a clear answer to the rich young man: "Go, sell what you own and give the money to the poor, and you will have treasure in heaven; then come, follow me." (Mk 10:21). We hear Jesus' challenge, but fight it. Peter's lament is often ours: "Look, we have left everything and followed you" (Mk 10:28). Isn't that enough? That is why we need to reflect regularly on Jesus' command to sell everything for the sake of God's reign. While the gospel promises great joy, it also makes painful demands.

The Sunday before Claire's departure, our family, her new fiancé and a few friends gathered in our living room. One of her sisters had picked a smooth stone from the garden to give to Claire. Each person first held the rock, rubbed it and prayed that all our love, concern and admiration would accompany Claire on her journey. Then we gave Claire the stone and told her to rub it whenever she felt lonely. It was a tender moment for all.

Claire's pilgrimage to Honduras became one of the most life-giving events in our family's faith development. Her letters about the people she met and the changes occurring in her because of their goodness reminded all of us to stop more often to hear one another's stories. Her commitment to accompany a people whose culture and language she knew only through books dared all of us to risk new adventures for the sake of the good news. And, she told us, only weeks into her year of service, that her rock had worn out. We had to send her another!

▸ *How do you send your family into the world with faith and hope?*
▸ *Who sends you?*

Sending one another in faith is a natural and necessary aspect of gospel living. Jesus spoke good news not just for us but for everyone. When we fail to send one another as good news, our message becomes stale and our family grows inward.

The gospel says it clearly: "Go into the whole world and proclaim the good news to the whole creation" (Mk 16:15). We are the message of God. We are the sacrament of Jesus. The quality of our faith relationships ought to be good news to all who are ready to hear. Still, we hesitate. Will we be unmasked so that all can see our weaknesses? Will we be rejected and pushed aside? The celebration of home rituals can attend to some of these fears, begin the process of healing and remind us that we are never alone. We go in Jesus' name. We are never alone.

Reflection

Although it is not always possible or advisable to take time immediately after rituals for conversation, nothing reinforces their transformative possibilities like common reflection. Discussions about what most touched, moved or confused us during the ritual allow everyone to let go of defensiveness and hold fast to the wonder of faith.

Moreover, because ritual prayer is new to most families, we can be overly sensitive to the slightest negative signs. People coughing or excusing themselves in the middle of the prayer can disturb the rhythm intended and become a distraction to all. That is why it is so important to reflect on our home celebrations regularly. These common periods of reflection give all present, even those who choose not to speak, an opportunity to test their assumptions and fears. More often than not, something that upsets one member has no effect on the others, but the opportunity to voice confusion or delight frees family members of unwarranted fears. Most importantly, the questions your family has will help refine future rituals while encouraging the active participation of everyone.

We feel sure you will be delighted by how much really goes on in your family's spirits when you gather regularly for prayer and ritual. While some members might not appear to participate in or enjoy ritual prayer, you might be pleasantly surprised by how much they are affected. Give everyone a chance to vent fears and frustration and growth is sure to follow.

In order to facilitate the process of reflection, we offer a series of questions at the end of each ritual.

So we begin. Notice again the simplicity of the process in making your own ritual wheel. Place INTENTION in the center. Choose actions for the next four movements—GATHERING, STORYTELLING, GESTURING, SENDING. Invite REFLECTION on what has happened.

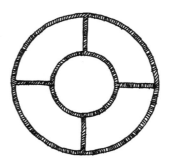

As your family continues to grow in experience and confidence in ritual making, you may want to add some more reminders to these suggested few.

A Few Reminders

Whenever possible, **clarify your intention** and **look over the ritual you have planned before everyone gathers.**

Choose the **most appropriate room** in your home for your celebration.

Choose **candles, flowers, an object from nature or a table covering** that draws everyone's attention and helps all **focus.**

The rituals in this book are models. **Feel free to adapt, shorten and change** them according to your particular needs. Initially, **keep them brief.**

Short vignettes precede every ritual. They allow families to see the importance of building rituals on experience. The four action steps proceed from the vignettes. However, **home rituals must reflect the reality of your family.**

When introducing rituals to your home, designate someone as a **leader.** Without someone to set the tone, home prayer easily flounders.

The use of **scripture,** while included in almost every ritual in this book, **is not mandatory.** At times, poetry, songs or favorite quotations might work just as well. Sometimes it is better simply to tell home faith stories.

Beginnings are very important. The leader can light a candle, ring a bell or invite all to take a few moments of silence to help families center themselves and make the transition to a new moment.

Endings are important, too. When the ritual is finished invite people to say: **So be it, so be it** or **Amen.**

Distractions are ordinary and often **unavoidable.** Be patient. There will always be someone who is uncomfortable. Rituals often do not work the way we intend. **Keep trying.** Your family is worth it.

CHAPTER 6

Types of Ritual

LIFE CYCLE EVENTS, GRIEFS AND LOSSES, and seasonal celebrations throughout the year seem to us to be the most important times when rituals help us name and value the past, plan for the future and live each day fully. When we take time to pause and mark where we have been, where we hope to go and accept ourselves as we are, we celebrate life as a continuum, a series of events some of which recur throughout our lives.

There are societies that take time to mark in ritual almost every significant event. They remember births, deaths, marriages, seasons of the year and so much more. We realize that most Americans are so busy these days that pausing to mark the major events of life is an effort. That is why we have chosen to offer the three major types of rituals that will follow.

Life cycle events, such as birthdays, baptisms and weddings, seem to us to be among the most important to celebrate through ritual. While many of these events are obvious and our society and church already mark them ritually, many others go almost unnoticed. These are events that affect almost every family, but because the feelings surrounding them are often unpleasant, we try to rush through or ignore them altogether.

Moving from the home of one's birth and settling into a new neighborhood, going to a new parish for the first time, puberty and menopause—these are all events that happen to us but go unmarked. In the rituals that follow, you will find many ways to celebrate these events. We are convinced that naming that which gives us pain is the first step in healing. Jesus said it this way: "Those who are well have no need of a physician but the sick do" (Mt 9:12). Admitting we are in need usually helps us experience personal peace and at the same time gain the courage to invite others to accompany us.

Experiencing everyday griefs and losses is another area too often overlooked in our families and societies. Going through a marital separation or divorce, failing important exams, and especially death are events that most of us prefer to ignore or deny. On the other hand, when we face them and move through them with compassion for all involved, we really need to celebrate.

For men in our society the loss of a job is an especially traumatic time. Most men continue to see themselves as defined by their work or jobs. When they are fired or laid off, even for reasons unrelated to job performance, they experience shame and guilt. Most of us also feel depression and lessening of self-worth. When we pause to experience these events on the level of feeling, identify with others who endured similar pain, and ask for the help not to run away, we almost always pass through these traumas with a renewed sense of hope and belonging in our families.

A close friend once said that just asking his family to pray with him the evening before he had to interview for a new job was a tremendous relief. He spoke of feeling their presence with him and around him throughout the next day. That his family also put a sign on their apartment door saying: "You're the best, Dad," caused his neighbors to think it was his birthday! Maybe they were right. My friend spoke of the events surrounding his firing and subsequent looking for work as a kind of rebirth.

The last section of rituals will focus on seasonal celebrations like Advent, Christmas, Easter and Thanksgiving. While many families already celebrate rituals for major feasts, we want to stretch your imagination and creativity. When rituals become too rigid, we fail to appreciate the story they try to tell. The rituals you will find in this book attempt to break some of the unnecessary boundaries we impose on ourselves with regard to family custom. We hope our suggestions will offer you ways to enrich your traditional family celebrations and inject your own ongoing faith story with new meaning.

Finally, at the end of most of the rituals you will find suggestions on connecting home rituals with parish life. While many families will be content simply learning new ways to gather, share stories and offer symbolic gestures of healing and transition, some will want to share their new prayer life with their parishes. We have cautioned families to be patient with themselves as they learn to be comfortable celebrating home rituals. Now we offer the same advice to families active in parish life. Be patient. Reclaiming your identity as churches and entering relationships of mutuality with your parishes is hard work. In most situations progress will be slow. Please don't get discouraged. Significant change is always slow. Trust your family's faith life and trust God.

LIFE CYCLES

BIRTHDAYS, BAPTISMS AND WEDDINGS are all examples of life cycle events that call for rituals. Most families bake and decorate cakes with candles to celebrate birthdays. Sometimes the cake even has one candle for each year of the person's life. Simple rituals like this remind the person celebrating a birthday that we really are lights in one another's lives.

Bill was eighty-eight was years old and living with his daughter and her family when he died. Easter came soon after the death. His daughter Paula was searching the linen closet for her family's bright yellow Easter tablecloth. Holding it up in front of her, she began to cry. Her dad's Parkinson's disease had caused him to drop and spill food regularly in his last years. The yellow tablecloth was badly stained. Thinking she would have to wash the tablecloth again, she brought it to the laundry where her eldest son was cleaning his shoes. When Paula told Todd about the tablecloth, the young man urged his mother not to remove the stains. He wanted to be reminded of his grandfather at their Easter dinner. Paula knew her son was right. Instead of washing the tablecloth, she placed a candle in the middle of the stained fabric and together at Easter her family lit the candle and prayed that their grandfather would experience the fullness of Easter light in heaven. It was a beautiful experience for everyone present and helped them trust that for those who believe "life is not ended but merely changed."[1]

Life cycle rituals are vitally important for the faith life of a family and a community. Rituals help us pause to celebrate joyful life cycle events as well as name and move through painful ones. Because Todd and his family were attentive to the everyday events of their lives, they were able to create a ritual that allowed them to grieve and rejoice simultaneously. Almost every life transition is full of opportunities for celebrating rituals. We have only to be attentive to these events to make them into times of authentic faith growth.

---

[1] *The Roman Missal*, Preface for Mass of the Resurrection.

While families rejoice at the birth of a child, they need also to attend to the radical new configuration of family structure each birth occasions. We remember Gaynell's son-in-law Tim saying that almost as soon as his daughter Sarah was born, everything changed in their home. The changes parents need to make when a child is born need prayerful attention every bit as much as the celebration of new life.

Morning Reflection

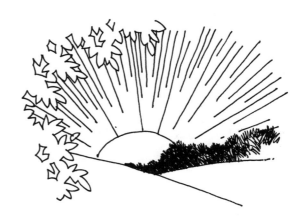

MAURA ALWAYS LOVED THE LIGHT of early morning. As a young girl, she recalled her father, who always was awake first, sitting in a chair drinking tea and watching the world come alive. Morning was quiet time for their family—a gentle slipping into the day.

Indeed, there was a marvel to night's passing which opened possibilities for the new day. Sleep, like a sacrament, had brought rest and healing to her tired body, spirit, and world while her morning shower would bless her body entering the day.

How she remembered savoring those morning moments! The aroma and first sip of freshly brewed coffee filled her with energy. The first breath of fresh air always cleansed and refreshed her as she stepped into the day. Her grandmother, she remembered, used to hum in the morning, saying this was the way she brought together the scattered parts of herself from sleep.

Her present family life seemed to begin on the run. As soon as she got out of bed and her feet touched the floor, she was waking children, fixing lunches, serving breakfast, and sending them off to school. She picked up even more speed as she dressed for her own day.

To help herself slow down, Maura created a morning body prayer as her personal gesture of uniting with others and greeting the new day. Observing her, the children began to pray with her. Together they developed an extended ritual which they do monthly. Daily anyone can do the body prayer alone or with others.

INTENTION Knowing she needed help to begin each day with a gentle rhythm, Maura wanted to design a ritual that would help her slow down.

In preparation for her ritual or yours we ask:

▶ *When do I sense myself going too fast and failing to pay attention to the wonder of each day?*

▶ *What ritual gesture might help me slow down, focus and appreciate the beginning of a new day?*

MATERIALS NEEDED: None

GATHERING	Say: "Ordinary day, let me know you for the treasure that you are, for in you is God." Then bow deeply from the waist.
STORYTELLING	The prophet Isaiah reminds us that God helps us listen (50:4):
	The Lord God has given me a well trained tongue, that I might know how to speak to the weary a word that will rouse them. Morning after morning God opens my ear that I may hear.
	We don't learn all at once. Every day we hear God's voice anew. Take a moment to ask: What shall we be taught today?
GESTURING	Stand straight and imagine yourself with deep roots extending down into the ground.
	Bring your arms up straight and reach to the sky.
	Take a few moments to image the circular movement of energy from earth to sky, from feet to hands.
	Stretch your arms out straight, shoulder-high, in a gesture of reaching to people everywhere who struggle. (Name needy people)
	Bring your open hands, one on top of the other, palms up to the space below your heart. Think of all those people who love you and give thanks for them.
	Then stretch your arms upward, hands together, gesturing outward into the day asking for an openness of spirit to whatever may happen in this day.
	Bring your hands together and bow deeply from the waist to reverence all of life.
SENDING	Sit quietly. Pray for the needs of people everywhere throughout the world, your own personal needs and those of your family.

REFLECTION Occasionally, perhaps on Sunday, share about how you feel when you slow down. How comfortable were you using the body prayer? What movement put you in touch with the day's needs?

Baby Shower

MARLENE AND HANK WERE SOON TO BE grandparents. When they first heard that their son and daughter-in-law were expecting, their family and some friends offered the couple and their newly conceived child a special blessing of protection. The meal at which they gathered was a time to remember how precious and fragile life was. Many told stories of different pregnancies, both easy and difficult. The sharing reminded everyone that we are not alone.

Now the family wanted to have a baby shower during which others could tell their own stories celebrating the journey to birth and new life. Because it was their first child, the couple needed baby clothes and articles. Most importantly they needed support as they prepared to raise a child.

INTENTION The invitation to the shower reminded the guests that baby clothes were needed and asked them to be prepared to share an important tradition from their past. It read:

> Alleluia:
> a time to remember . . .
> a time to share . . .
> Take a moment to recall the birth of your child
> or a special child in your life,
> and a favorite
> story you read,
> nursery rhyme you spoke,
> song you sang,
> tradition you began
> or experience you remember,
> and bring it to this shower.

In preparation for this celebration or yours, we ask:

▸ *Who should be invited? Do you want men present?*
▸ *What gesture will help all recall the wonder of pregnancy, birth and the raising of children?*

MATERIALS NEEDED: Enough ribbons for each person present, with a word expressing a quality of living, e.g. peace, joy, gentleness, compassion, etc. A cup or glass filled with juice.

GATHERING   Friends and family surprise the mother-to-be with this shower. People form a circle around a low table in the living room. In the center of the table is a blessing cup or glass and ribbons arranged like the spokes of a wheel.

STORYTELLING   As each gift is opened, people share their favorite story, nursery rhyme, song or experience.

For example, one woman read a story from her childhood, *The Little Engine That Could,* and spoke of how it had sustained her through difficult times.

Another woman spoke of her rocking chair and the security and calm it brought when her children were restless, crying or angry.

Another woman actually sang the song she had whispered to each of her children when putting them to bed at night.

Another woman recited each of her children's favorite nursery rhymes and remembered how important they felt when she read these poems to them.

Another woman with no children of her own brought a recipe for ice cream that she had made weekly for the neighborhood children.

After all have had a chance to speak, someone reads:

The Acts of the Apostles reminds us that anything is possible when we share (2:43–47):

Awe came upon everyone, and many wonders and signs were done through the apostles. All who believed were together and had all things in common; they would sell their possessions and divide them among all according to each one's needs.

GESTURING   The cup of blessing is held up:

Leader: For the blessing of children and those who care and nurture them, we give thanks. We mingle our lives in the raising of children, knowing that as our African friends say: "It takes a whole village to raise a child." We taste of the goodness of life and the privilege that is ours to respect and reverence all of life.

(The cup is passed in silence. Everyone sips from it.)

SENDING   The expectant mother thanks all for coming and sharing their strength and care. Each person is invited to draw a ribbon from center and reads whatever is written on it.

For example, "I will try to bring _____ to all children and my family."

Hugs are given to the expectant mother and all present.

REFLECTION   What do you most remember about people's kindnesses when you were expecting a baby?

Do you have a favorite thing to do when you hear that people you know are expecting a child? What is it?

PARISH   Parishes might offer blessings and prayers for expectant mothers at least quarterly. When the entire parish is invited to share the wonder of new life, hope for the future of all is enhanced.

Birth

Eduardo and Concepcion were vital and energetic members of their community and church. They seemed to have enough time for everyone, especially those most in need. At the same time, they carried a heavy burden. They were unable to conceive. They had spent untold hours and money on tests and trials trying to discover what they might do to have a child. Nothing worked.

That is why they were overjoyed and immensely proud when they learned they were pregnant. Though anxious throughout the pregnancy, their faith consoled them during the nine months of waiting. When Angela Maria was born they were overwhelmed. They had waited ten years for a healthy birth, and they wanted to celebrate their joy with family and friends, especially people they had met at the fertility clinic which had so helped them. They knew that a carefully planned ritual could assist them in showing their gratitude to God and all those who had accompanied them during their years of waiting.

INTENTION Eduardo and Concepcion need to express the joy and thanks they feel for their new-born daughter. Because so many people have been praying with and for them, they do not want to celebrate alone.

To celebrate their ritual or yours we ask:

▸ *Who should be invited to celebrate new birth?*
▸ *What gestures will help everyone know how much his or her support means?*

MATERIALS NEEDED: Polaroid camera (if possible) or a book where people can write their names, a small loaf of bread or a large roll, a simple dessert.

GATHERING   After everyone gathers, the mother begins.

Mother: Thank you all for coming. May I ask you to gather in a circle around us? The Polaroid camera is set up and we want to take a picture of all of us to hang on our child's crib (picture is taken). [Or] Would you please sign your name in this book?

We want ___(name)___ to be surrounded by the faces ___(names)___ of all those who have loved us during these many years of waiting. We want our baby to know love, not just ours but all of yours as well.

STORYTELLING   All present are invited to speak of some person in their lives who has been food for them and how they hope ___(name)___ might always have people in his or her life to nourish him or her.

Listen to a reading from the gospel of John (6:35, 48–51):

> Jesus said to them, "I am the bread of life. Whoever comes to me will never hunger, and whoever believes in me will never thirst . . . I am the bread of life. Your ancestors ate the manna in the desert, but they died. This is the bread that comes down from heaven, so that one may eat of it and not die . . . Whoever eats this bread will live forever."

GESTURING   After each person speaks, he or she breaks and eats a piece of bread.

Parent: We probably will never be able to tell you how grateful we are that you have been with us but we want you to know how much we love you. (Husband and wife feed each other with the last of the bread.)

SENDING   Those present gather around the baby and softly sing Happy Birthday. All then share a simple dessert.

REFLECTION   What do you remember best about your children's infancy? What do you think is the most important gift you can give newborns?

PARISH   While parishes already light candles for newborns during the baptismal ceremony, we suggest an extra candle be lit in our parish churches every time another child is born. The candle(s) might be lit during the prayers of the faithful.

Baptism

BAPTISM CAN BE AMONG THE MOST MOVING OF religious experiences. While most parishes celebrate baptisms joyfully, we can enhance baptismal celebrations even more by beginning and ending the celebration with home rituals.

Tim and Claire wanted to introduce their first-born to their parish family with real gladness. Tim's background was Methodist and Claire's was Catholic.

INTENTION Although Sarah would be baptized in the Catholic Church, Tim and Claire wanted to find a way to honor both of their religious denominations. They also wanted to affirm Sarah's grandparents and remind themselves that Sarah would surely grow strong in faith and love the deeper they recommitted themselves to one another in marriage.

In order to prepare for their celebration and yours we ask:

▸ *How can we help people realize how important they are to us?*
▸ *What gestures might best demonstrate our gratitude and hope?*

MATERIALS NEEDED: water from grandparents' homes, wedding candle, camera, favorite foods, cup with newborn's name and date of baptism.

The following ritual is divided into three parts. The first and third are at the home of the new parents. We hope that families will try to celebrate all three sections but realize that circumstances may make this impossible.

At Home Before the Baptism

GATHERING

Parents, grandparents, godparents and friends gather the evening before the child's baptism. They form a circle around a table that holds two small carafes of water. Next to the water is the couple's wedding candle.

STORYTELLING

First parent: Thank you all for coming. You have been such an important part of our lives that baptism of ___(name)___ would be incomplete without you. We hope you know how much it means to us to have all of you here (lights wedding candle). You have always been lights in our lives.

Second parent: For now, we want to pause and ask you to remember someone in our family who has influenced you. Then, saying something like: "I sign you with Uncle Albert's generosity," each of us will sign ___(name)___ with the cross and pray that he or she will have all the gifts of our family.

(All sign the baby with the cross, praying that the child will be gifted with the qualities of the person who meant so much to them.)

First parent: We have asked our parents to bring water from their homes. We were refreshed by their love and faith throughout our lives. We ask them now to mix the waters together and ask you to extend your hands over these waters and bless them. We'll bring their waters to our parish baptismal font and mix them with the waters of our church during the baptismal ceremony, praying that our mingled faith will always strengthen ___(name)___. Now listen to the words of the psalmist:

A reading from Psalm 139:

> Lord, you have probed me, you know me; you know when I sit and stand, you understand my thoughts from afar. My travels and my rest you mark; with all my ways you are familiar. Even before a word is on my tongue, Lord, you know it all. Your formed my inmost being; you knit me in my mother's womb, I praise you, so wonderfully you made me; wonderful are your works!

Second parent: Thank you so much for coming. We pray for you and bless you with gratitude.

(The people named as special in this ceremony can be mentioned in the litany of saints during the baptism in the parish church.)

Church Baptism

A. In addition to the ceremonies celebrated in every parish setting, we suggest parents and godparents ask the parish staff about the following rituals.

Parents carry their lighted wedding candle in procession and light the paschal or Christ candle from it, saying:

We give great thanks to Christ who is our light. We have known his light in our marriage and want to share it now with our new-born __(name)__ .

B. One or both of the godparents read the scriptures.

C. Many couples use the prayers of the faithful from their wedding ceremony, especially if they composed them, at baptisms.

D. The names of the people mentioned as role models for the newborn in the home ritual are included in the prayer of the faithful.

E. Before the blessing of the waters the celebrant says:

I invite the grandparents of __(name)__ to mix the waters of their homes in our baptismal font. (Grandparents pour water into font.) Because they have shared love and compassion with their children, we want their grandchild __(name)__ to be washed in these same gifts.

F. A simple cup inscribed with the newborn's name and date of baptism is used to pour the waters of baptism. As soon as their child is able to drink from a cup, he or she uses it daily.

G. The final blessings for mother, father and assembly are offered by all.

   1. All mothers join in blessing the mother.

   2. All fathers join in blessing the father.

   3. All in the church bless the couple and their family.

At Home After the Baptism

After the ceremony in the parish church, all return home to bless the food, take pictures and tell stories.

REFLECTION   What does baptism mean for your life today?

What and/or who has been your biggest support in faith?

Engagement

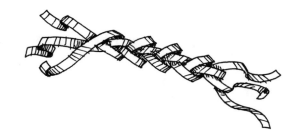

ALTHOUGH THEIR ENGAGEMENT WAS EXPECTED, when Meaghan and Matt made the formal announcement their families were excited and full of joyful congratulations. The young couple's friendship had grown over the last year into a desire to spend their lives together.

The flurry of planning for a wedding began almost immediately—where to have the reception, whom to invite, what food to serve, which dresses to wear. It was easy to get caught in the busyness of planning. Meaghan's sister, remembering her own engagement, wanted to take time to celebrate and welcome her sister's fiancé into the family.

INTENTION Everyone wanted to offer a wish, a prayer and a hope for Matt and Meaghan.

In preparation for their celebration or yours, we ask:

▸ *Who should be invited to the engagement party?*
▸ *What gesture will help express the excitement and hope all wish for the newly engaged couple?*

MATERIALS NEEDED: two candles, three ribbons for braiding attached to a marriage cross, braided bread, bells.

GATHERING Any children present ring bells as friends and family members gather in a circle around a small table in the living room. Two candles are lit.

One is lit for Meaghan in gratitude for her presence in her family's life as daughter, sister, friend. The second candle is lit for Matt in thanksgiving for his presence as son, brother, friend.

STORYTELLING Each person is invited to speak of a special wish or hope for the engaged couple and braid the three ribbons on the table.

Sister: We have braided our hopes together for you as a gift that all our lives might become more connected in the sharing of hearts and families. Now we ask you to listen to St. Paul's first letter to the Corinthians and remember your own gifts (1 Cor 12:4–7):

There are different kinds of spiritual gifts but the same Spirit; there are different forms of service but the same Lord; there are different workings but the same God who produces all of them in everyone. To each individual the manifestation of the Spirit is given for some benefit.

GESTURING   The engaged couple together hold up the braided bread and pray:

"May our lives continue to be braided together in gentleness and peace.

"May this bread nourish us in our commitment to one another and to you as family."

The bread is broken by the couple and passed around the circle. When everyone has a piece, all say "So be it" and eat.

SENDING   The completed braid of ribbons and the cross are given to the couple as a remembrance of their decision to braid their lives together with the shared hopes of their family and friends.

Some couples place the cross and braided ribbons around their wedding candle at their marriage.

All present extend their hands in a blessing over the couple as someone prays:

"May you grow together each day as an image of Christ who is one with us forever."

The leftover bread is taken outside and offered to the birds, a sign of sharing our life with all creation.

REFLECTION   What are your fondest memories of your engagement?

PARISH   Parishes might offer a special blessing for the engaged three or four times a year. It would be very encouraging for most parish communities to meet those planning to be married in their church. The couples receiving the blessing would also get a sense of the concern and prayer of the people in their parish.

Wedding Shower

CECILIA AND THE OTHER BRIDESMAIDS, together with the mothers of the bride and groom, wanted to plan a shower for her sister. In talking about the shower, the married women remembered what a wonderful sign of affirmation their shower was and how it gave them essential things one needed to begin a new home. Even more importantly, showers were a time for women to speak of their experience of home, family, and their relationships as mothers, grandmothers, wives, aunts.

Cecilia remembered her grandmother embroidering flowers on pillow cases and telling her to place them in her hope chest. She smiled at the memory; young women didn't have hope chests any longer. She also recalled the recipes her grandmother gave her and the Saturday she spent at grandma's learning to make beignets (French donuts). Her grandmother was determined to send her into marriage with a grounding in her French heritage and cuisine. Grandma wanted Cecilia not to worry about gathering with her family and friends for festive meals. Even though her husband did most of the cooking, Cecilia had shared her grandmother's recipes with him.

Cecilia suggested they ask the people invited to this shower to bring a family custom, ritual or tradition that was still part of their home life today, something that helped them to remember and name who they were as family. In this way everyone could pass on the importance of family rituals and traditions and invite the bride to consider ways to develop family rituals with her husband.

INTENTION The women preparing the shower wanted to affirm the newly engaged couple's desire to marry, offer them gifts they could use each day, and share stories and rituals that meant so much in their own lives.

In preparation for this celebration or yours, we ask:

- *Who should be invited? Is this a good time to expand showers to include men?*
- *What gesture(s) might affirm the newly engaged woman or couple and help them focus on the awesome mystery of marriage?*

MATERIALS NEEDED: invitations to the shower asking everyone to bring a tradition, custom or ritual from their family or culture. Punch and ingredients for a simple meal.

GATHERING	As the newly engaged woman enters the house, all her friends, seated in a circle, welcome her. The basket of gifts is placed before the bride to be.
STORYTELLING	As each gift is opened, the person giving the gift shares her story of her chosen tradition, custom, ritual.
	For example, we eat corned beef, cabbage and potatoes on St. Patrick's day and read Irish tales. The children love the stories but dislike the cabbage.
	After all share, someone reads:
	Matthew's gospel reminds us that Jesus will always be our companion (28:5, 20):
	Do not be afraid . . . I am with you always, until the end of the age.
GESTURING	The newly engaged woman serves everyone punch from a common bowl. All toast one another in honor of the traditions that speak of who they are as women and as family.
SENDING	All offer the engaged woman a blessing of fearlessness. This gesture, with roots in India, though given without words, has a clear meaning: May you have nothing to fear from me, nor I from you.
	Blessing of Fearlessness: Extend the hand gently toward the engaged woman, fingers together and upright. Remain in this position for a few seconds.

REFLECTION   What tradition or ritual moved you most today? Explain.

First Wedding Anniversary

EGGY AND ROBERT ARE PLANNING their first wedding anniversary celebration. It has been the most powerful and at times the most difficult year of their lives. Bob travels at least one full week a month. Peggy is teaching in a new school and returns home late each afternoon, torn. Marriage was difficult for her in ways she never expected. She had lived alone for four years after college and loved her own company. She never thought she would resent Bob's coming home to their apartment. When she did, she felt guilt.

It was also a wonderful time. She and Bob often lingered over meals, read to each other, took long walks, even went to dancing class. They wanted everyone, especially their parents, to know how grateful they were for the support they received and celebrate with them the gratitude they felt for a wonderful first year of marriage.

INTENTION Peggy and Robert want to be very honest about their first year of marriage. They want to be grateful for the good times while not denying the struggles they experienced.

In preparation for their celebration or yours, we ask:

- *Whom do we invite?*
- *How do we tell people how much they mean to us?*
- *What action can we use to symbolically express our deepest values?*

MATERIALS NEEDED: music, wedding photo, unlit wedding candle, two unlit candles, bottle of wine or juice.

GATHERING   Two young married couples as well as their parents and siblings gather with Peggy and Bob. Beethoven's Ninth Symphony, or whatever song the couple chose for the recessional at their wedding, plays in the background as everyone gathers. (Their wedding photo and candle sit between two unlighted candles.)

Wife: Thank you, God, for my husband and our parents who formed us in faith. (She lights a candle.)

Husband: Thank you, God, for my wife and our friends who challenged us to grow in faith. (He lights a candle.)

STORYTELLING   The couple shares how each has become a light for the other. Then read:

A reading from the gospel of Matthew (5:14–16):

> You are the light of the world. A city built on a mountain cannot be hidden. Nor do they light a lamp and then put it under a bushel basket; it is set on a lampstand where it gives light to all in the house. Just so, your light must shine before others, that they may see your good deeds and glorify your heavenly Father.

Please share with us who has been a light in your lives.

GESTURING   *Couple:* Because of you our first year of marriage, though difficult at times, was wonderful. You taught us how to grow, change, adapt and mostly love. We hope we can all return for one hundred years of celebration. (The couple relights their wedding candle from two other candles.)

Couple: Thank you for being light for us. We love you and pray that our marriage may be a light for others.

SENDING   Music plays as all go to dinner which features a bottle of wine or juice saved from the wedding meal. Before everyone leaves, all join hands to pray in hope for the year to come.

REFLECTION During the meal everyone is invited to share his or her favorite moment from the wedding day.

If appropriate, ask the question:

What do you think is the most important element of a successful marriage? How do you speak honestly of the difficult times in marriage?

PARISH At least one Sunday a year parishes would do well to recognize married couples in the general intercessions, invite all to renew their marriage vows and ask the oldest and youngest couples to present the gifts. They might also serve donuts and coffee to mark all anniversaries.

Welcome Home Birthday

ELAINE HAD BEEN OUT OF THE COUNTRY for four years. A warm, gentle woman, she had stayed in close touch with her family but had not celebrated a birthday at home the entire time. Her mother, for whom her children's birthdays were very important, wanted Elaine to know how much she was missed and so planned a lavish affair. Elaine got word of the plans and became very uncomfortable. She shared with her mother how little the people had in the Central American country where she had lived. Together, after realizing that they had made many assumptions about what this birthday celebration would be like, they planned the following ritual.

INTENTION   Elaine's family, trying to be sensitive to her concern for the poor, want to welcome her home for a birthday celebration with great joy and simplicity.

To celebrate their ritual or yours we ask:

▸ *Who ought to be invited? Are there people from the country where Elaine served in the area?*
▸ *What gesture will express our love simply and joyfully?*

MATERIALS NEEDED: music, a decorated empty chair, a bell, a bowl of clean water on the table, food for simple meal.

GATHERING   Latin American or other appropriate music plays as all gather. When everyone is seated, a small bell is rung.

Birthday person: In ____(country)____ the church bell is rung to call the people to church. I am so happy to be back in our "home church."

STORYTELLING   *Parent:* Dear daughter, we are so proud of you. We've missed you terribly. Each year you were away, we gathered on your birthday, left an empty chair and prayed you were happy, healthy and living your dream of working among very poor people. We invite you now to sit with us again in this special chair.

Friend: Dear friend, I have missed you so much. Though we wrote often, not knowing the fullness of what was happening to you was a great loss. So I want to read from Paul's letter to the Romans (8:31–33, 35, 36–39):

> If God is for us, who can be against us? He who did not spare his own Son but handed him over for us all, how will he not also give us everything else along with him? . . . What will separate us from the love of Christ? Will anguish, or distress, or persecution, or famine, or nakedness, or peril, or the sword? No, in all these things we conquer overwhelmingly through him who loved us.

People are invited to speak about what it has been like not having the birthday person in their lives.

GESTURING   *Birthday person:* As I drink this sparkling clear water, I pray for all of you without whose love and confidence I could never have gone away. I also pray for the people of ___(country)___ who rarely have clean water. I am so happy to be home. (Drinks water, then passes it for all to drink.)

SENDING   *Friend:* O God of all longing and wonder, without you nothing makes sense. Thank you for accompanying us through the darkness of birthday celebrations that seemed empty without ___(name)___. Because you are with us, we gather today with greater joy than ever. Our sister, daughter and friend who was away has come home. We will always be grateful for her witness.

(The bell is rung again and all sing Happy Birthday.)

REFLECTION   All then partake of a simple meal of bread, rice, soup and cake during which we ask: Have you ever spent a birthday alone? What was it like?

Birthdays

BIRTHDAYS ARE TIMES OF JOY AND CELEBRATION. Even if it only means we are a year older, a birthday reminds us of our uniqueness as human beings and children of God. In many cultures, bells are rung on birthdays, wishing happiness in the years to come.

From her earliest years, Bonnie remembered her mom celebrating her birthday with her favorite meal and a chocolate cake with double chocolate frosting. Everyone played pin the tail on the donkey, ran in a three-legged race, joined in a scavenger hunt and dropped clothespins in a bottle. She also recalled the time her mother invited the children to make birthday hats, using their own designs, drawings and favorite colors. Everyone was curious to see what the others had made. Wearing a hat made you feel festive. Birthdays were great fun.

Bonnie also remembered playing games at her children's birthdays. Only later did she discover that her kids always joked with the neighborhood children about their mom making everyone a winner. She did try to promote cooperation over competition but she guessed it hadn't worked as well as she thought.

INTENTION When she reflected about her family, Bonnie knew they all still needed affirmation. She wanted all of them to know of their own goodness and that they counted. She loved giving gifts but sometimes it seemed that buying gifts had become a substitute for honestly finding a way to say how much that person meant in your life. Then she remembered her mother encouraging the children to make hats. She decided to create a ritual of the birthday hat.

Instead of buying a gift, she asked all family members to choose and draw a sign of how they experienced the person celebrating a birthday during the past year. A big floppy hat with a wide brim or band sits in the middle of the table. After each person draws their sign or symbol, they place it on the hat. After the meal, the celebrant puts the hat on his or her head, reaches up blindly to take a symbol, unfolds it and shows it to everyone. The person who drew the symbol explains why he or she chose that particular symbol to describe the celebrant. For example, a person might draw an eye and say: "You seem to be seeing all of us in a gentler way this year and I really admire you."

Each person present describes his or her symbol to the celebrant. In Bonnie's home, they no longer buy gifts. The birthday hat with its rich symbols is gift enough.

To prepare for their celebration or yours we ask:

▶ *What symbol best describes the person celebrating a birthday?*
▶ *Draw the symbol you choose on a small piece of paper, fold it and place it on the birthday hat.*

Materials needed: a large hat with a brim or band, paper for signs, bells, candles and cake.

GATHERING   (bells ring)

Leader: We are thankful for the parents who gave ___ (name) ___ . life, for sister(s), brother(s), grandparents and relatives who nourish that life.

STORYTELLING   After the hat is placed on the birthday person's head, he or she takes a sign from the hat. Its meaning is explained by the person who crafted it. After everyone shares, someone reads:

Psalm 36 reminds us that God is a fountain of life and light (Ps 36:6, 9):

> Lord, your love reaches to heaven; your fidelity, to the clouds. We feast on the rich food of your house; from your delightful stream you give us drink. For with you is the fountain of life, and in your light we see light.

GESTURING   *Leader:* We light these birthday candles in honor of ___ (name) ___ who has been your light to others. Without ___ (name) ___ our world would not be the same: we as family would be different. ___ (Name) ___ is a gift for us all. Through this candlelight we remember the birthdays of all present. It is good to be alive!

All sing Happy Birthday.

Leader: ___ (Name) ___ , inhale the breath of the Spirit around us. Then exhale and blow out the candles, sending your own breath-spirit to all the earth.

SENDING   Family members kiss and hug the birthday person and say "I love you."

Bells are rung.

REFLECTION   If you could design any birthday celebration you wanted, what would it be like? Do you know of customs that other families use for birthdays that you would like your family to consider?

PARISH   Each month parishes might want to mention the names of those celebrating birthdays. If the list is too long, they could post the pictures of people celebrating birthdays that month in the entrance way of the church. They might also want to invite children to bring bells from their homes and ring them for the gathering rite of the mass.

Blessing a New Home or Apartment

THE LEGERE FAMILY TRIED TO SETTLE INTO their new home. Packing and unpacking seemed a forever process. Finally, they felt as though they were home again. Though it was not easy to leave their old home and neighborhood, they were grateful to the family who had sold them their new home.

Even though they were mostly settled in their new home, there were a few problems. Warren, their six year old, was anxious about sleeping in his new room. Grandma Legere, who lived with them, found the steps to the second floor new and difficult. Everyone experienced new smells and unfamiliar sounds. Thank God, Beverly was already searching for new friends. Her energy brought laughter and joy to the entire family.

Because their transition was not as easy as they anticipated, the Legere's decided to create a ritual that would help them honor their former home, bless their new one and pray for a bright future.

INTENTION The Legere family wants to bless their new home and each of its rooms. They also want to express their need for a safe and secure emotional and physical space for family growth. In letting go of the past, while acknowledging its beauty, they want to open their door again in welcome and hospitality to God and others. Finally, they want to renew their conviction that all space is sacred when we gather in God's name and ask God to fill it.

In preparation for their celebration or yours we ask:

- ▸ *Whom do we invite to the house blessing?*
- ▸ *What gestures will help us let go of the past and welcome the new?*
- ▸ *What feelings do you associate with moving?*

MATERIALS NEEDED: mulled cider, dried herbs and flowers, ribbons, bells and a wreath.

GATHERING   Parents and children gather in the kitchen which has always been the heart of their home. Mulled cider brews on the stove. The foundation for a wreath of dried herbs and flowers is in the center of the table. Extra dried herbs and flowers are ready to be tied together with ribbons for each door.

STORYTELLING   As people tie dried herbs and flowers with a ribbon and place them on the family wreath, they speak of what they want their new home to be. After all share, someone reads.

The prophet Isaiah reminds us that everyone wants to live a safe life in a peaceful home. He writes (Is 32:17–18):

> Justice will bring about peace; right will produce calm and security.
> My people will live in peaceful country, in secure dwellings and quiet resting places.

(A minute of quiet follows.)

GESTURING   Together, in silence, the family walks from room to room ringing bells softly, spiritually cleansing each room. A bunch of dried herbs is affixed to each door as they go. Returning to the kitchen, they open the door as a sign of welcome to all people and creation.

Eldest child: Peace to our house and all who enter here. May the Lord preserve our going out and coming in.

Anyone who cares may add a prayer. Then the newly made wreath is fastened on the door.

SENDING   After all toast with and drink the cider, the mother prays:

> God of this home, bless our new dwelling place.
> May peace and joy abide here and may goodness and mercy live here.
> May the calm light of patience and courage shine here.
> And into our homes may we welcome all people and creation in a spirit of love and hospitality.

All: Amen.

REFLECTION What will you miss most about your old home and neighborhood? What do you look forward to most about your new home?

▶ *This family continues to bless their home each year by inviting friends and family to an open house on New Year's eve.*

PARISH Parishes reconsecrating their churches or welcoming a new pastor might ask families to bring herbs from their home to make a parish wreath of welcome. A prayer for the parish and world is said as the wreath is placed on the door of the church.

A First Day of School and Birthday

(Multicultural)

FRANCISCO AND HEATHER SANCHEZ had four children. When their youngest, Cynthia, was preparing to enter school for the first time, they wanted to celebrate her transition and theirs. Since her birthday was August 15, they decided to use this occasion to celebrate her new birth into school.

Francisco was born in Mexico, Heather in southern California. Because of the different cultures from which they came, their marriage had sometimes been painful. They wanted the ritual not only to mark Cynthia's passage into school but to remind their family of the goodness of their diverse cultural background. They invited both sets of grandparents, Cynthia's closest Mexican American and Anglo friends and her kindergarten teacher. Francisco asked his parents to bring some soil from Mexico. Heather, whose parents had moved to northern California, asked her parents to bring soil from their garden and from the redwood forest. The ritual that follows will work in any multicultural setting.

INTENTION Francisco and Heather, knowing how difficult it can be to live in a bicultural marriage, wanted to find a way to acknowledge the difficulty and celebrate the challenges of cultural diversity.

To celebrate their ritual or yours we ask:

▸ *Whom should we invite to a gathering like this?*
▸ *What gesture will help us experience the wonder of multicultural life?*

> MATERIALS NEEDED: music, soil from grandparents' place of birth, family perennial plant or bulb, birthday cake and candle.

GATHERING	Appropriate national music plays in the background.
	After everyone is present, the leader begins.
STORYTELLING	*Parent:* Welcome. We are very glad you are here. Today is not only a birthday but a final opportunity to celebrate with everyone from our families before our youngest daughter goes to school for the first time.
	Sibling: ___(Name)___, sometimes it's hard to come from two cultures. People can be mean. We pray that you will always be welcomed in school.
	Sibling: ___(Name)___, school is difficult at times but also lots of fun. We pray that you will learn a lot and be very happy with your new friends.
	Parent: ___(Name)___, soon you will go to school. This is what Jesus says to help us remember we are never alone (Mt 19:14):
	Let the children come to me, and do not prevent them; for the kingdom of heaven belongs to such as these.
GESTURING	*Parent:* Mom and dad from ___(country of origin)___, mom and dad from ___(country of origin)___ would you bring the soil you brought and mix it with the soil of our family perennial. (Soil is mixed and, if possible, the new perennial is planted.)
SENDING	*Grandparent:* Happy birthday, ___(name)___. Next year on your birthday we hope we'll all share wonderful stories of your first year in school.
	(Mother lights candles on cake and begins singing Happy Birthday, first in English, then in the language of the culture which her child shares.)

REFLECTION   What has been your greatest joy living in a multicultural family?

PARISH   Parishes, especially those with multicultural communities, would do well to bless the children before the first day of school in all the languages of those present.

Welcoming a Child's New Friend

Seven year old Brendan entered a new school in September. Making new friends was very important to him. He asks his mother if he can invite his new friend Gavin to a meal at his home. Listening carefully to Brendan's excitement, his mother calls Gavin's mother and inquires about a good time for a meal visit. She also asks Gavin's mother to send Gavin with a favorite toy, planning to use it in a ritual of welcome.

INTENTION Changing schools and neighborhoods has been very difficult for Brendan. His parents want to recognize his struggle, honor his fears and help him celebrate finding new friends in school.

To celebrate their ritual or yours we ask:

▸ *Whom should we invite, if anyone, to welcome Brendan's new friend?*
▸ *What gesture will help young children live well in a new environment?*

MATERIALS NEEDED: favorite toy of each child, new toy or game to share, food for a meal.

GATHERING　　When Brendan's family gathers for supper, Gavin is told he can pick any place at the table he really likes and that Brendan will sit next to him. After they choose places to sit, Brendan's mother puts Brendan's favorite toy in front of him and asks Gavin to do the same with his favorite toy.

STORYTELLING　　*Parent:* God, we're happy to welcome ___(friend's name)___ to our home as ___(son's name)___ new friend and we pray you will bless us as a family with new friends.

GESTURING　　(after all have eaten)

Parent (I): ___(Friend's name)___, will you tell us why this is your favorite toy?

(Friend answers.)

Parent (II): ___(Child's name)___, would you tell us about your favorite toy?

(Child answers.)

Parent (I): We have a new toy for the both of you which we thought you could share. ___(Friend's name)___, we want you to know that whenever you visit us this toy will be here for both of you. Thank you again for being ___(son's name)___ friend.

SENDING　　After sharing dessert one parent says:

We hope you come back to share many meals with us.

REFLECTION　　Adults might discuss what they do to manage change in their lives.

Breaking Bread Meals

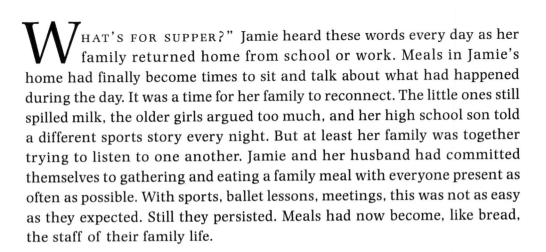

WHAT'S FOR SUPPER?" Jamie heard these words every day as her family returned home from school or work. Meals in Jamie's home had finally become times to sit and talk about what had happened during the day. It was a time for her family to reconnect. The little ones still spilled milk, the older girls argued too much, and her high school son told a different sports story every night. But at least her family was together trying to listen to one another. Jamie and her husband had committed themselves to gathering and eating a family meal with everyone present as often as possible. With sports, ballet lessons, meetings, this was not as easy as they expected. Still they persisted. Meals had now become, like bread, the staff of their family life.

INTENTION Jamie and her husband wanted to introduce their family to regular prayer at meals. They hoped a few moments of quiet and reflection would enhance a peaceful environment for family conversations. They planned to ask their children to pray formally only once a week. To their surprise, the children enjoyed praying and even asked that some part of the ritual be included at each family meal.

In order to prepare for their ritual or yours we ask:

- *How often should we pray before meals?*
- *What occasions call for special prayers?*
- *What gestures might help families recognize how important their gatherings are?*

MATERIALS NEEDED: unsliced loaf of bread or a single slice of bread on a plate, bells.

GATHERING   As the family gathers around their table, the youngest children ring bells.

This is a signal for all to become quiet.

STORYTELLING   *Leader:* We thank you, God, for health, food, shelter, vigor and forgiveness. We thank you for people who love, care and rejoice in the gift of life fully lived. We thank you for all the gifts of creation.

St. Luke tells us that people recognized Jesus in the breaking of the bread (24:35–36):

> Then the two recounted what had happened on the way and how he was made known to them in the breaking of the bread. While they were still speaking about this, he stood in their midst and said: "Peace be with you."

Let us hold hands and pray our individual thanks or needs.

GESTURING   *Leader:* Bless this meal and bless the people who share this meal. This is a holy place and we are holy people.

(Someone holds the bread up. In silence, the bread is broken in half and passed around.)

Leader: We share this bread as we share our life.

SENDING   *Leader:* We thank each family member for the gift of life he or she has given us. We extend a thank you by offering a sign of peace and saying to one another: (Name)   , thank you for being in my family.

Bells ring. Meal begins.

REFLECTION   Share a custom or practice that you experienced with another family.

Alternatives for Different Meals and for Storytelling

- ▸ *Thank each family member for something he or she has done in the past week that has benefited the family.*
- ▸ *Thank others for personal qualities that they possess and that are appreciated.*
- ▸ *State something about yourself that you like.*
- ▸ *Name a quality of the family that is precious, that helps in life and that the person speaking would like to receive more of in the coming weeks or months.*

Blessing Cup Meal

THE ERNST FAMILY SEARCHED for a way to express who they were and to celebrate life. They gathered for Christmas, Thanksgiving, Easter, birthdays, anniversaries and holidays. These were festive times and offered a sense of belonging, but they wanted something to help them mark every day. Their lives were so busy that clearing off the kitchen table was more challenging than setting it. They also wanted to find a way to gather the diversity of interests and involvement the family had in the community. The Ernsts shared many things in common and wanted a way to express this at mealtime.

INTENTION After talking with one another, the family decided they needed to give thanks for the past, for people who loved them through all the ups and downs of life: grandparents, relatives, friends, teachers and all who continued to be lights for them. In their name they would light a candle to the past. They also wanted to light a candle to the future to help them see the way ahead with hope. Between these two candles, they place a blessing cup filled with a favorite beverage. It symbolizes the present and represents the family's day mingled together.

The blessing cup has become very important to the Ernsts. They use it on all important occasions as well as on those days when a family member wants to announce or share something special that happened that day.

MATERIALS NEEDED: blessing cup or glass, two candles.

GATHERING   Family sits around the table. In silence a candle is lit to the past. (pause)

Then a candle is lit to the future. (pause)

STORYTELLING   Each person then has the opportunity to speak of his or her experience of the day.

All hold hands as someone reads:

Listen to St. Paul speak to the Corinthians (10:16a):

> The cup of blessing that we bless, is it not a participation in the blood of Christ?

GESTURING   The blessing cup is held up.

Leader: As we pass our blessing cup, we thank God for all the people in our family. As each person drinks from the cup, thank God in your heart for that person and pray for his or her needs.

(Cup is passed in silence)

SENDING   At the end of the meal, the family can warm their hands by the candle of the past or the future, whichever seems most important at the time. They might also extend hands over one another in blessing, praying that all will help create a world of peace, justice and belonging. Sometimes what remains in the cup is poured into the earth as a way of sharing family blessings with all of creation.

REFLECTION   Which family member has been the biggest blessing to you recently?

▸ *When the blessing cup is passed to honor or help one person, the leader ought to mention that person's name in the ritual—e.g. "As we pass the blessing cup, we thank God for (name) and all the people in our family."*

Young Man Entering Puberty

JAMIE ALWAYS WANTED TO BE OLDER. His brother Guy turned fifteen and talked about nothing except getting his driving license. Guy seemed so grown up. Wanting to be like his older brother, Jamie learned the driver's manual even before Guy. His parents recognized Jamie's desire to be treated more like an adult. As his thirteenth birthday neared they planned the following ritual.

INTENTION   Jamie's parents want to help him name and celebrate his emerging manhood.

In preparation for Jamie's celebration or yours we ask:

▸ *How do we let children know we recognize their growth?*
▸ *What gestures will help adults and parents celebrate these new realities?*

MATERIALS NEEDED: scrap or photo book, camera, two candles, shaving cream, razor.

GATHERING   Jamie's best friend, Alex, his grandparents, siblings and parents gather in Jamie's home. Because his parents want to emphasize the formal nature of this event, they invite everyone into the dining room. The dining room table has a scrap book of Jamie's earliest photos and is opened to a blank page marked **ADOLESCENCE**. The photos taken at this party will go into the photo album marking Jamie's passage from childhood into his teen years. (If a scrap book is not available, choose signs for different periods of growth and transition in a boy's life.)

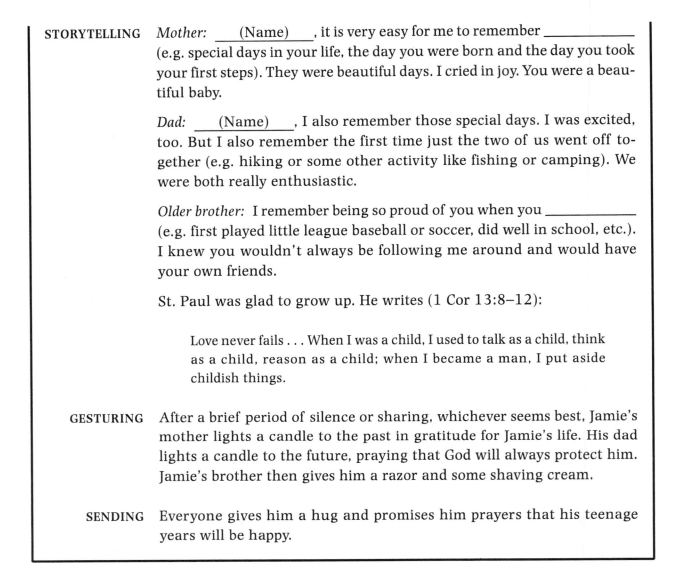

STORYTELLING *Mother:* ___(Name)___ , it is very easy for me to remember _____ (e.g. special days in your life, the day you were born and the day you took your first steps). They were beautiful days. I cried in joy. You were a beautiful baby.

Dad: ___(Name)___ , I also remember those special days. I was excited, too. But I also remember the first time just the two of us went off together (e.g. hiking or some other activity like fishing or camping). We were both really enthusiastic.

Older brother: I remember being so proud of you when you _____ (e.g. first played little league baseball or soccer, did well in school, etc.). I knew you wouldn't always be following me around and would have your own friends.

St. Paul was glad to grow up. He writes (1 Cor 13:8–12):

> Love never fails . . . When I was a child, I used to talk as a child, think as a child, reason as a child; when I became a man, I put aside childish things.

GESTURING After a brief period of silence or sharing, whichever seems best, Jamie's mother lights a candle to the past in gratitude for Jamie's life. His dad lights a candle to the future, praying that God will always protect him. Jamie's brother then gives him a razor and some shaving cream.

SENDING Everyone gives him a hug and promises him prayers that his teenage years will be happy.

REFLECTION All share about their best and/or their most difficult memories of becoming a teenager.

Young Woman Entering Puberty

WITH THE ONSET OF MENSES Madeline felt that she had entered another phase of her life. Finally, she was like everyone else. So many of her friends already had had their first period. When hers was delayed, she was fearful there was something wrong with her. Even though her mother, who had her first menses for three days before talking with anyone, assured her that she was fine, Madeline was concerned.

At the same time, she was not prepared for the new and unfamiliar feelings in her body. She felt as if everyone was noticing her. Despite her mother's sensitivity, she was embarrassed about her new experiences. With everything about her so different, she did not know how to act or what to do.

Surprised by her fear, since she had anticipated this event for the past year, she began to wish it would go away. At the same time, she was fascinated by her new self. Finally, she decided to speak with her grandmother. Together they prepared the following ritual.

INTENTION Madeline's grandmother assured her that it would be good for them to gather with her mother and aunt to share memories of their entrance into womanhood. She wanted Madeline to learn to honor and listen to her body.

In preparation for Madeline's ritual or yours we ask:

▸ *How can we learn to attend to and accept new experiences in our lives?*
▸ *What gestures might help us pass through transition times gracefully?*

MATERIALS NEEDED: tea, candle.

GATHERING   To bless this new beginning, Madeline, her mother, grandmother and aunt gather for tea on a Sunday afternoon.

STORYTELLING   *Grandmother* (lighting a candle): As we strike this match we light and warm the memory of what it was like for us to experience our first period and what has happened to us because of that event. (Each person has the opportunity to speak.)

Mother: When women are together over a long period of time, they experience the same monthly cycle. We pray in gratitude for women everywhere who support and affirm one another in this life giving process and listen to the book of Psalms (143:8):

Remind me each morning of your constant love, for I put my trust in you. My prayers go up to you. Show the way I should go.

GESTURING   God who loves us like a mother is also our friend. Let us share tea as a sign of God's love and our friendship.

SENDING   The older women extend and warm their hands from the candle and together bless Madeline with light and warmth. All embrace.

REFLECTION   Share the feelings you had during the ritual. What most touched you?

Leaving on a Trip

TRIPS OR JOURNEYS, especially those which mark a significant milestone in a person's life, are important to mark ritually. A graduation trip to Europe, a sending into mission service, and moving to a different part of the country all call for a ritual to remind the persons going that, like a tree, they have roots and branches and can depend on their friends, families and communities to accompany them in spirit when they travel.

Ever since finishing college, Claire had planned to work in a third world country. She wanted to experience what it meant to live with very little and discover ways to be involved with the poor for the rest of her life. Her parents and siblings, while supportive of her dreams, were also frightened for her. The place where she planned to serve had almost no clean water and was ruled by a military dictatorship. While Claire would be serving far from the cities where clashes regularly happened, communication was difficult. There were no phones and mail took at least two weeks to be delivered.

INTENTION Because they wanted to acknowledge their fears and celebrate their joys, Claire's family designed the following ritual.

In preparation for her celebration or yours we ask:

▸ *How do we tell people our deepest hopes and needs?*
▸ *How do we symbolically express our desire to leave and take people with us at the same time?*

MATERIALS NEEDED: candle, rock.

GATHERING   After a supper of the departing person's favorite foods, her family and closest friends gather in the family room in a circle. In silence her mother lights a single candle.

STORYTELLING   *Leader:* Listen to a reading from the gospel of Matthew (7:24–25):

> Everyone who listens to these words of mine and acts on them will be like a wise man who built his house on rock. The rain fell, the floods came, and the winds blew and buffeted the house. But it did not collapse; it had been set solidly on rock.

Now I ask you to share how we can be a rock for ____(name)____ .

For example, one promises to be a rock of prayer for her. A second friend, her boyfriend or fiancé, reminds her that their relationship was built on the rock of deep love and will survive her year away.

GESTURING   A sibling tells all that she has taken a small stone from the family garden or other appropriate place.

Sister or brother: Dear sister, I am going to pass this stone around our circle of family and friends and ask all of them to rub all their hope, love and affection for you into it. (The stone is passed.)

Please accept this stone as a sign of our love for you.

SENDING   *Best friend:* Dear friend, whenever you really feel lonely, scared or in need of extra help, take out your newly blessed stone. Rub it and remember all of us here today who go with you in spirit.

All hold hands in silence, then approach the young woman and offer her an embrace.

REFLECTION   If there is time, share on the questions:

Who have been a "rock" in your life? When do you most remember them?

PARISH   Parishes might gather up this ritual by composing a sending prayer and blessing for lay missionaries or others beginning a new ministry.

Returning from a Trip

BILL AND HIS BUDDY STEVE HAD BEEN PLANNING to drive cross-country ever since the seventh grade. Their parents finally agreed to help finance their odyssey after graduation from college. In each place they stopped for more than a few days they sent postcards to their families. In this way, everyone had a chance to share their excitement and occasional troubles. When they were only a week from arriving home, their parents got together and prepared the following ritual of welcome.

INTENTION   The parents of Bill and Steve wanted their sons to know how much they were missed while they were away as well as help them make the transition to home.

In preparation for their celebration or yours we ask:

➤ *How do we tell adult children they are missed?*

➤ *What is an appropriate gesture to offer newly graduated young people who have been on the trip of a lifetime?*

MATERIALS NEEDED: welcome banner or sign, music, postcards, garland of flowers.

GATHERING   Two family members prepare a banner of welcome. Together they wait outside the house in order to be the first to greet the travelers. Both sets of parents, and as many siblings as possible, gather in one of the traveler's homes. The young people's favorite music is playing and their postcards are pinned to the front door.

STORYTELLING   *Leader:* Welcome home! We missed you very much. Even the dog seemed lost without you. We're glad you're safe and well and we're anxious to hear your stories of adventure. But first let us listen to God's word (Deut 6:20–26):

> Later on, when your son asks you what these ordinances, statutes and decrees mean which the Lord, our God, has enjoined on you, you shall say to your son, "We were once slaves of Pharaoh in Egypt, but the Lord brought us out of Egypt with his strong hand and wrought before our eyes signs and wonders, great and dire, against Egypt and against Pharaoh and his whole house. He brought us from there to lead us into the land he promised on oath to our fathers, and to give it to us."

After reading he says:

So tell us what you found in your promised land. Tell us about your trip, especially what most touched or moved you.

GESTURING   After the travelers speak, people share how they feel about their return. All embrace and a simple garland of flowers (already prepared) is placed around each traveler's neck.

SENDING   The young people's favorite meal is served. Before eating, all hold hands and each person prays in gratitude for the travelers' return and the adjustment all will have to make now that the trip is over.

REFLECTION   What was the most important and/or enjoyable trip you ever took? What were your most difficult problems and/or greatest excitement?

Menopause

Aᵂᴼᴹᴬᴺ ɪꜱ ᴄᴏɴꜱɪᴅᴇʀᴇᴅ ɪɴ ᴍᴇɴᴏᴘᴀᴜꜱᴇ when she has not bled for one year. For Rosemary there had been some unpleasant symptoms: hot flashes, depression, mood swings and a feeling of being lost. She knew that some of her friends had had similar physical experiences. For others the difficulty was in letting go emotionally and grieving for what once was. Fear came for Rosemary when she acknowledged that she was growing and looking older. She had new aches and pains, tired easily and often felt lonely.

At the same time, Rosemary knew that menopause was a time of initiation into a new phase of her life. She had recently become a grandmother for the first time and the deep respect and love she had for her own grandmother came flooding back to her. Her grandmother was such a wise woman. She wanted the gift of wisdom for herself. In a paradoxical way being a grandmother and entering menopause at the same time was a gift. Her sister reminded her that many cultures considered women after menopause wise elders who were expected to be the community's voice of responsibility toward children and the earth. She would have the opportunity to say no to anything that did not serve life. Her grandmother had been a wise woman for her. Perhaps she could offer her new wisdom to others. But first she would have to find a way to embrace menopause.

INTENTION Rosemary wanted to enter menopause in a positive way by honoring her child-bearing years while reverencing what was now beginning.

In preparation for her celebration or yours, we ask:

- *How does one name the loss that menopause brings?*
- *What qualities of the wise woman do you already have?*
- *What gestures will help name one's fears and reach for understanding?*

Mᴀᴛᴇʀɪᴀʟꜱ ɴᴇᴇᴅᴇᴅ: photos, shawl, incense, instrumental music, milk flavored with honey, vanilla, cinnamon.

GATHERING   When inviting her sister and some friends to her home, Rosemary asked them to bring a picture of themselves at puberty. The photos would help them remember so much of what happened in their lives and what was happening to them now. She placed the photos in the middle of the table with a new shawl and lit some incense. The women sat quietly around the table imagining the incense cleansing their spirits of doubt and fear as they inhaled and exhaled. Instrumental music played softly in the background.

STORYTELLING As each woman showed her picture, there was much laughter. Then they spoke about what had happened to them since the picture was taken. They spoke, too, of their fears of dealing with the negative and misunderstood aspects of menopause. After everyone speaks, someone reads.

Listen to the wisdom of Sirach (6:27–28):

> With all your soul draw close to her; with all your strength keep her ways. Search her out, discover her; seek her and you will find her. Then when you have her, do not let her go; Thus will you afterward find rest in her, and she will become your joy.

GESTURING   Someone, preferably an older woman or sister, drapes the shawl across the shoulders of the newly menopausal woman and says:

God clothes us in compassion and walks with us always.

SENDING   Milk flavored with pinches of honey, vanilla, and cinnamon is poured into cups for all to drink and passed clockwise to reflect the setting sun. The woman entering menopause toasts all present with words of nourishment:

May the calcium in this milk be a symbol of the extra strength we need for the rest of life's journey.

REFLECTION   What and who have been your greatest strengths during other transitional periods of your life?

Share ideas about diet, health issues and exercise.

Helping the Elderly Let Go

TERESA WAS IN HER EIGHTIES and about to move to Florida to be closer to one of her daughters and grandchildren. Her husband had died thirteen years ago and she had grown increasingly lonely. Her other children wanted to send her with joy and hope while not denying the pain all feel in moving to a new home.

INTENTION   Although many people had been a part of Teresa's long life, her children wanted their mother to sense her immediate family's love. They chose to celebrate this intimate moment with their mother alone. (If your circumstances differ, you may choose to invite extended family.)

In preparation for her celebration or yours we ask:

- *How do we let go of important people and send them to new possibilities?*
- *What symbolic action can we use to express our love?*

MATERIALS NEEDED: earth, lily bulb or flower, water.

GATHERING   All gather in Teresa's dining room, a place she has made holy by the hundreds of meals she has served her adult children there. One child has taken some earth from their father's grave. It sits in the middle of the table with a lily bulb next to it. The lily was the last gift Teresa's husband Joe had given her before his death.

STORYTELLING   *Oldest child:* Mom, we want to send you in peace to (place—e.g. Florida). Your work may be finished here with us but you have an entire new life to enjoy. We are grateful for all you did for us.

This reading from the book of Proverbs reminds us of you (9:1):

> Wisdom has built her house, she has set up her seven columns; she has dressed her meat, mixed her wine, yes, she has spread her table.

Each tells a story for which he or she is most deeply grateful.

GESTURING   *Second child:* As we plant this flower in the soil from dad's grave we pray that dad will be your companion on this new step you are taking. We promise you our prayers as well.

Third child (pouring water on the plant): We water this plant for you in gratitude for the joy and refreshment you have brought to our lives.

SENDING   Mother is offered the opportunity to say a few words if she likes.

For example, Thank you all for coming. Although I leave in sadness, I know that what I am doing is better for me at this stage of my life and ask you to continue to remember me to God when you pray.

The children then package the newly planted flower for shipment to their mother's new home and prepare a meal of her favorite foods.

REFLECTION   Afterward all share favorite memories of their mother, father and family meals. Children might also share how they have taken the values and customs of their parents into their own homes.

GRIEF AND LOSS

PERHAPS NOTHING CALLS ON OUR FAITH as deeply as grief and loss. Divorce, especially for Christians, can be very disturbing and conflicting. Catholic Christians insist that marriage, as a reflection of Christ's love for the church, must be forever. How to call on our faith when divorce becomes inevitable is a very important question. Even when there are grounds for annulment, the people involved feel guilt, anger, loss and so much more. We need to learn to pray about these events at home as well as in our parish churches.

How wonderful it would be for neighbors to come together without taking sides and pray with couples who have decided that divorce is their only option. After all, most of us realize that separation and divorce can come to anyone. How to let go of the emptiness of failure, attend to the children involved and move on in life is a critical task for many home churches.

Another painful but often ignored loss in our society is miscarriage. Women, especially if they have chosen not to speak publicly of a new pregnancy, can feel painfully alone when they miscarry. A young couple of our acquaintance even spoke of their friends telling them they should be relieved since they already had two children. Faced not only with a lack of compassion but rejection of their loss, they withdrew from family and friends for months. Only when they spoke to their children about the miscarriage did they find the understanding and sympathy they craved.

The loss of a job is another event many people suffer. Without warning, companies find themselves in deep financial difficulty. Workers, even long term employees, have to be fired. To be among those let go can be devastating. I was a newly ordained priest living in New England in the early 1970s. The aerospace industry, which employed thousands of women and men, began to stumble badly. The Franco-American community was especially hard hit. Not only did our parish experience a loss of revenue in our collections, but many people were so ashamed that they stopped attending church on Sundays. Not to notice these chilling events would be an affront to the gospel. Especially at home, we need to learn to name and pray about our griefs and losses.

Miscarriage

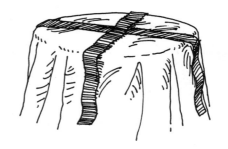

THERE WAS LIFE GROWING INSIDE HER. Marion was only in the first trimester and few people knew she was pregnant. When she and Albert shared the news with their children, they were very excited. The miscarriage came so suddenly. What happened? Did she do something wrong? Had she not cared properly for herself? Marion felt the loss deeply.

A few weeks passed but the sadness continued. Marion found herself crying unexpectedly over the least thing. One day she noticed the date she had marked on the calendar for the child's birth. Sorrow enveloped her.

It was difficult to explain what she felt inside. When her youngest son prayed each night that his deceased grandfather take care of his baby, Marion knew she needed to talk with other women who had experienced something similar.

INTENTION Despite the pain she felt, Marion did not want to deny her need or move too quickly through her grief. Still, she needed compassion. She had several friends who had miscarried. She yearned for their understanding and hope. She also wanted to bring their strength to her grieving husband and children.

In preparation for her ritual or yours we ask:

▸ *How do we ask people to share something as painful as a miscarriage?*
▸ *What gesture might help Marion name and begin to pass beyond her grief?*

MATERIALS NEEDED: ribbons, pansy or other perennial flower.

GATHERING
Marion invited three women friends and her grandmother to her home. They gathered around a table divided into four sections by a flat ribbon. Each section represented a direction of the earth. In the table's center Marion placed a flowering pansy, a perennial, to represent life that blooms each year.

STORYTELLING
Woman who has miscarried: I know each of you has already experienced the loss of someone in your life. Even though I did not know this child as I know you, I was deeply aware of life growing inside me.

(If she is able, she speaks spontaneously of her loss. Then all are invited to speak of their own sorrow. Finally, someone reads.)

Listen to the wisdom of Ecclesiastes (3:1–3):

> There is an appointed time for everything, and a time for every affair under the heavens. A time to be born, and a time to die; a time to plant, and a time to uproot the plant. A time to kill, and a time to heal; a time to tear down, and a time to build.

GESTURING
After sharing, the women knew they were not alone in their grieving and wanted to connect themselves with women everywhere who had similar experiences.

Each placed their hands in one of the four sections of the table indicating a direction of the earth.

Then they prayed for women of north, south, east and west who had experienced loss. After their prayer, they took the perennial and planted it in the yard.

SENDING
Standing in a circle around the newly planted perennial, the women held hands and prayed. Through their touching hands, they imagined sending strength to one another. Then stretching out their hands, they sent their strength to women everywhere.

REFLECTION   If time permits, all gather around the table and share:

Which women in your life most encouraged you to grow in faith? Explain.

A later addition:

Marion's son noticed the perennial and asked about it. As she explained, she realized that her son, husband and daughter were also struggling with loss. The entire family gathered for a conversation about their sorrow. A few months later, while turning a page on the calendar, Marion noticed a pansy drawing on the month in which the baby would have been born. It was her son's drawing.

Together as a family they planted a flowering tree, a sign of the importance of life and the acceptance of God as living in all of life, even in loss.

Facing Failure

MARIA, HAVING FAILED TO SCORE HIGH enough on the entrance exams to get into law school, decides to invite her friends to a party of gratitude for their support during the time she studied for the exams. She invites her parents and siblings, and her grandmother who has always been a special source of strength to her, as well as her boyfriend and her closest friends. In preparation for the party, Maria asks everyone to bring a symbol of failure in his or her life.

INTENTION Maria wants to help herself and everyone joining her to honestly face failure with hope.

In preparation for her celebration or yours we ask:

▸ *How do we learn to tell the stories of personal failure? What do they feel like?*
▸ *What gesture will help us express gratitude for the support we experience despite failure?*

MATERIALS NEEDED: signs or symbols of failure, circle of candles.

GATHERING When the guests come through the front door of Maria's apartment, they are met with a sign reading: Today is the first day of the rest of your life!

All gather around a circle of unlit candles and share about the symbol of failure they brought. Maria asks her grandmother to speak first.

STORYTELLING For example, *Grandmother:*   ___(Name)___ , in searching through my memories I remembered an unfinished baby sweater that I had been knitting when I was pregnant with my fifth child. You know I miscarried him after four months. I was brokenhearted for a while. Then I realized I had more time to give my love to your mother and her two sisters and brother. That really helped me snap out of my hurt.

Father: I brought a basketball to remind me of not making the high school varsity team. I thought I'd die. Then you became a wonderful player, Maria, and my joy was doubled.

Brother: I brought my report card from second grade. We were new to this country, my language skills were weak and I had to repeat second grade. It was humiliating but really good for me. Besides I met my best friend Ray that year and we've been through a lot together.

Friend: Maria, I brought a friendship ring that my first boyfriend gave me. I have never been able to give it away till now. I want you to have it as a sign of our friendship and a promise to be friends through everything.

Boyfriend: Dear best friend, today I brought the strings of my old guitar. When I was in high school I wanted to be a professional musician. For a long time I couldn't believe I didn't have the talent. The string is broken but my love for you isn't. I'm glad to be here.

When all have shared, someone reads:

St. Luke tell us that we need to die in order to live. Listen (8:5–8):

> "A sower went out to sow his seed. And as he sowed, some seed fell on the path and was trampled, and the birds of the sky ate it up. Some seed fell on rocky ground, and when it grew, it withered for lack of moisture. Some seed fell among thorns, and the thorns grew with it and choked it. And some seed fell on good soil, and when it grew, it produced fruit a hundredfold." After saying this, he called out, "Whoever has ears to hear ought to hear."

GESTURING After a period of faith sharing or silence, each lights a candle of hope from the circle which has been placed on the coffee table around which they have gathered. All ask for strength to get through disappointment and recommit themselves to one another in friendship.

SENDING All join hands and promise to be a support for one another in good times and not so good ones.

REFLECTION If appropriate, ask the questions:

Who helped you get through difficult times in your life? Have you ever been privileged to help others in this way?

Divorce with Dignity

Emily had been divorced from Tim for three years after fifteen years of marriage. Although they both worked hard to protect their three children from unnecessary hurt, their parting was painful and occasionally angry. Emily kept a journal regularly after her divorce. In it she recorded hurts and angers but also her dreams. She knew she had to find a way to keep her dreams alive if she would ever feel whole again.

INTENTION Searching for a deeper peace especially after Tim remarried, Emily asks her three closest friends to share a ritual with her in which she will try to bury her past and begin again.

In preparation for her celebration or yours we ask:

▸ *How do we express the suffering of divorce and separation we feel?*
▸ *What action can we use to symbolically express letting go of the past?*

MATERIALS NEEDED: journal (notes), matches, pot, soil, edible herb.

GATHERING After all have gathered, Emily invites her three friends into her bedroom. Since her divorce, she has used it as a place of study, reflection and prayer. All pause for a few moments, never sitting down but surrounding Emily in a small circle. Emily picks up her journal.

STORYTELLING *Wife:* This journal (these notes, scraps of paper, etc.) contains so many of my thoughts, feelings, fears and dreams. After my divorce, I tried to be as honest as possible with God. And God was honest with me.

Listen to what Jesus says in the gospel of John (12:24):

> Amen, amen, I say to you, unless a grain of wheat falls to the earth and dies, it remains just a grain of wheat; but if it dies, it produces much fruit.

Please share how you survive great loss. For example, one friend shares how dying and suffering led to new hope for her.

Friend: Please pray with me and respond: Help them, gracious God.

For all divorced people and their children that healing may come to their families. *(Response)*

For all people trapped in bad marriages that they may find a new path. *(Response)*

For those preparing for marriage that they may realize that healthy relationships are hard work. *(Response)*

For divided families, especially those who see no way to help themselves. *(Response)*

GESTURING   Together all go outside to burn the journal (notes, etc.). The divorced person mixes the ashes with soil and pots the ashes and soil with an edible herb that will be used frequently in cooking. The divorced woman then invites all her friends to return in three months when she will use the newly grown herbs to help prepare a meal for them.

SENDING   The women exchange signs of peace and courage and promise to pray for one another.

REFLECTION   If time permits, all share on the questions:

What was the most difficult thing I have had to let go of in my life? Who most helped in the process? Have I been able to help others?

Forgiving

WITH SO MUCH PRACTICE it had become a pattern in the Williams family to avoid conflict and pretend that everything was O.K. But sometimes her children's whining "It's not fair!" consumed Martha's energies. Teasing and ridicule were becoming a daily occurrence, or so it seemed. When she found herself responding with angry and unkind words she knew she had hurt others and upset herself.

Yesterday her family had a heated argument. While her family all regretted the things said, the leftover feelings permeated the hearts and atmosphere of their hurting home.

Sometimes the heaviness of her family's tension left Martha too exhausted to sleep. Because her husband Larry did not seem as bothered by the family strain, Martha felt even more isolated. Her feelings of abandonment reminded her of her childhood, making it very difficult to ask for or offer forgiveness.

INTENTION   Martha wanted to find a way to let go of old resentments and admit present ones. She sensed her family's desire to do the same.

In preparation for her ritual or yours we ask:

▸ *What family situations unfailingly inflame our anger?*
▸ *How can we name them honestly and let go of them through gesture?*

MATERIALS NEEDED: two candles, slips of paper.

GATHERING	After telling everyone she wanted to create a peaceful environment for healing, Martha and her family picked an evening when all could be present. As they gathered, two candles were lit—one to the past and one to the future. Between the candles was a container with slips of paper.
STORYTELLING	*Leader:* I want to invite each of you to take a slip of paper and write down those situations which always upset you. When you are finished writing, please feel free to share with us what you have written. Then put your paper in the container. (Pause)

John's letter reminds of God's forgiveness. Listen (1 Jn 1:9):

> If we acknowledge our sins, God is faithful and just and will forgive our sins and cleanse us from every wrongdoing.

May I now ask you to share how you might avoid the words or tones of voices that upset you and others.

GESTURING	*Leader:* In order to heal our family wounds, let's try this breathing exercise.

Breathe in and out gently; let the wounds of family hurt surface. Breathe in light to bathe our family wounds with life's goodness. Breathe out the healing light to each member of the family.

Using the candle of the past, all burn the papers on which are written situations that upset them.

SENDING	Together the family extend their hands to the candle of future for warming. Each person embraces every other person present.

REFLECTION   Share a moment of healing you experienced in our family about which no one knows.

PARISH   This ritual can continue in our parish churches, especially during Lent. On the last Sunday of Lent, families bring papers with hurtful words or tones of voice. The papers can be burned as part of the penitential rite.

Ending a Friendship

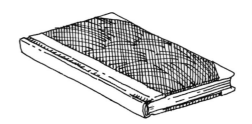

HOW CAN A FRIENDSHIP END? How do we break relationships? At the thought of not seeing her friend again, tears welled in Louise's eyes. What had she done? Not done? She felt terrible. Her sense of self-worth was shattered and life seemed bleak. She had strong feelings of rejection, of being pushed aside, even abandonment. Some days she felt frozen and unable to move on with her life. Like a child who made a mistake, she blamed herself and seemed unable to stop the tears.

Her friends reminded her that forgiveness and healing take time. But they didn't understand. Her anger toward her friend, herself and God was too deep even to begin that process. Why had this happened? She wanted to understand and heal.

Because her friendship had grown over a long period of time, the process of releasing and letting go would be gradual. Writing in a journal helped. Louise wrote about her thoughts and feelings. Sometimes she even drew them.

INTENTION Louise wanted to let go of something precious with honesty. She knew she needed a way not to deny her hurt while trying to remain positive toward life.

In preparation for her celebration or yours we ask:

▸ *With whom, if anyone, should Louise gather at a time like this?*
▸ *What gestures might help her pass beyond hurt toward healing?*

MATERIALS NEEDED: journal or notes, seeds for sprouting and a jar.

GATHERING | Deciding to celebrate this ritual alone, Louise lit some incense and began her breathing prayer. With every inhalation she imagined drawing in a healing light. With every exhalation she let go of anything that was threatening her.

She asked:
What am I feeling inside right now?
What is keeping me from feeling at peace?

Breathe in love, breathe out resentment.
Breathe in forgiveness, breathe out grudges.
Breathe in peace, breathe out anger.
Breathe in happiness, breathe out sadness.

She focused on the area inside most in need of healing. Resting in the unhealed space, she opened herself to any thoughts, feelings, images or words that came.

STORYTELLING | After trying the above exercise, write in your journal or draw regularly, every day if possible. Then read (Mk 4:26–29):

> Jesus said, "This is how it is with the kingdom of God; it is as if a farmer were to scatter seed on the land and would sleep and rise night and day and the seed would sprout and grow, he knows not how. Of its own accord the land yields fruit, first the blade, then the ear, then the full grain in the ear. And when the grain is ripe, he wields the sickle at once, for the harvest has come."

GESTURING | By keeping a journal and reflecting on the scriptures Louise stumbled on a symbolic gesture that reflected her feelings. You may wish to try something similar.

Placing sprouting seeds in a jar, Louise soaked them every night, rinsed and drained them in the morning, and repeated this process over a few days. Finally, the seeds began to crack, as did her feelings. When the sprouts emerged, she put them in a jar, placed them in the sun and waited for them to turn green.

SENDING | Louise invited her friends to her home for a meal and put the sprouted seeds in a salad. Together they ate from her friendship bowl.

REFLECTION | This reflection works best when saved for a later time. What new seeds are growing in your life? Who nurtures them?

Praying for Someone Who Is Ill

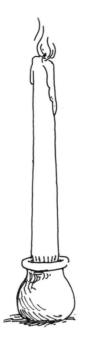

M Y NIECE KETT WAS DIAGNOSED with childhood leukemia when she was three. After we heard this shocking news, the distance between our home and my sister's seemed to stretch far beyond two thousand miles. We were on the phone constantly—what doctor, what hospital, what protocol? We cried together and raged against the uncertainties of life.

In my home, I noticed that family members were not faring too well. Everyone seemed reluctant to speak, to share feelings. Before a Sunday meal someone suggested that we name a candle for Kett, and place it on the table. Before the evening meal, Kett's candle would be lit and people would simply sit quietly in its light imaging Kett whole and healthy again.

This simple gesture continued over the next few months. People were faithful, quiet, and responsive. Finally, in my curiosity to discover why this prayer seemed to work so well, I asked if anyone would like to suggest a reason. My son, usually a very quiet man, replied immediately. "That's easy, Mom. I simply picture God sitting in a rocking chair holding Kett, rubbing her arm the way you used to do when we were sick, telling her everything will be OK. Isn't that what everyone sees?"

I realized then how important our images of God are during healing times. Here was a picture of a compassionate God, holding and rocking a child into health. So many memories came to me. I saw again my mother holding me in her arms providing me with a sense of security and protection. And I remembered holding my own children as I sat in the old rocking chair to which I moved when I was sad and hurting.

INTENTION   Everyone in my family, feeling the helplessness of not being able to do anything directly for Kett or my sister's family, wanted to find a way to remember Kett prayerfully each day. At the same time, since we would repeat this ritual often, we did not want too many words. In this ritual, therefore, storytelling, except for a reading from scripture, is put aside. The gestures are our prayer.

In preparation for our prayer or yours we ask:

▸ *How can we be honest with ourselves, God and our family in a simple prayer for someone who is ill?*

▸ *How can we symbolically express our deepest feelings?*

MATERIALS NEEDED: chime or bell and a candle.

GATHERING   (A chime sounds)

Leader: We listen to our hearts, O Lord, and the sound of your presence within and among us. May the space inside our hearts and around those gathered at this table be open to your healing presence. Help us understand your word in the letter of James (5:13–15):

STORYTELLING   Is anyone among you suffering? He should pray. Is anyone in good spirits? He should sing praise. Is anyone among you sick? He should summon the presbyters of the church, and they should pray over him and anoint [him] with oil in the name of the Lord, and the prayer of faith will save the sick person, and the Lord will raise him up. If he has committed any sins, he will be forgiven.

GESTURING   A candle is lit. The person striking the match ought to bring the flame to the wick gently as if he or she were bringing the light of Christ in each person to the candle.

Leader: In quiet, image ____(name)____ whole and healthy again.

SENDING   *Leader:* Imagine the light filling you, this place, our world, and ask God to surround ____(name)____ with the light. In the strength and power of your healing presence, Lord, we stretch out our hands and send your warm and healing light to ____(name)____ who is ill.

REFLECTION   On occasion, share the images and feelings that came to you about the sick person during the ritual. Is anything different now in you? Is there a shift in feeling and/or understanding? What is your image of God?

PARISH   Families can bring candles from their homes to be used during the rites of the anointing of the sick. Parishes might also remember the sick by lighting a candle for each sick person during the general intercessions.

Anniversary of a Death

G RANDMA ANNA HAD BEEN WIDOWED fifteen years when she died at eighty-five. Her four children all found her very helpful at different times in their life. After her death, they gathered in a large group with their own children and grandchildren and asked the simple question: If you had to pick one word to describe grandma, what would it be? Four words came up over and over again in the conversation. They were: loving, family, listener, generous. To mark their mother's death in a personal way, her children crafted a prayer cloth to be used in a ritual in her honor. They also decided to use the cloth each year to mark their mother's anniversary.

Although the following ritual is quite specific, it can easily be adapted for use in any family.

INTENTION Anna's children did not want her to be forgotten. More importantly, they wanted the values she lived to become a part of their families' lives.

In order to celebrate their ritual or yours we ask:

▸ *When is the best time to gather so that the most people in the family can be present?*
▸ *What gesture will help all to remember Grandma Anna and reinforce the families' commitment to her values?*

MATERIALS NEEDED: music, a piece of cloth with four symbols drawn on it reflecting grandma's values, magic markers. Placed on this remembrance cloth later: a cross (from casket or home), grandma's favorite flowers, a candle, her picture.

GATHERING   Grandma's favorite music or hymn plays. In silence, the four youngest grandchildren enter the room carrying the remembrance cloth and place it on a table. Already drawn on the cloth are four symbols which represent their grandma.

STORYTELLING   *Leader:* Today we gather to honor and remember our mother, grandmother, great-grandmother, mentor and friend. We want to take a few minutes to tell you four things about her. We have chosen these symbols which speak of the way she lived her life.

Grandchild: First we drew a heart. This says how her (quality, e.g. humor) touched all of us with love.

Grandchild: Then we drew an ear. This says how her (e.g., wisdom) moved all of us to listen well and carefully to one another.

Grandchild: Then we drew a circle of stick figures. This says how her (e.g., faith in us as a family) kept her positive about life even when she suffered.

Grandchild: Finally we drew a basket of bread. This symbol says how she (e.g., loved to cook for large crowds) and always managed to care for the very poor.

Each person then has an opportunity to draw a word or symbol of their love for grandma on the remembrance cloth. When completed, people share the meaning of their symbols and how they intend to live out grandma's values in their own life. Finally, someone reads:

Listen to how God loves us (Song 2:10–14):

> My lover speaks; he says to me, "Arise, my beloved, my beautiful one, and come! For see, the winter is past, the rains are over and gone. The flowers appear on the earth, the time of pruning the vines has come, and the song of the dove is heard in our land. The fig tree puts forth its figs, and the vines, in bloom, give forth fragrance. Arise, my beloved, my beautiful one, and come! O my dove in the clefts of the rock, in the secret recesses of the cliff, let me see you, let me hear your voice. For your voice is sweet, and you are lovely."

GESTURING   In silence, a cross, grandma's favorite flowers, and her picture are placed on the remembrance cloth. A candle is lit. These remain on the table for the meal that follows.

SENDING   All join hands and pray the Lord's Prayer. Food of some special meal grandma liked, e.g. meatballs and spaghetti, grandma's specialty, is eaten.

REFLECTION   How do you see yourself bringing grandma's faith to your family and community?

PARISH   On the anniversary of death, the names of the deceased are mentioned in the general intercessions. The remembrance cloth could drape the eucharistic table for the presentation of gifts.

Death of an Abusive Person

BILL HAD BEEN TOUGH ON HIS CHILDREN. While everyone tried to understand the pressure he felt working two jobs and never having enough money, he often drank too much, got loud, fell asleep in the middle of dinner and verbally abused his kids for not doing better in school and life.

INTENTION   Bill's three children loved him and wanted a way to let go of the hurt they felt in order to remember the good things he did and tried to do for them and their mother.

In order to celebrate their ritual or yours we ask:

▶ *Is this the right time to try to heal our family from the abuse we felt?*
▶ *If it is, what gesture(s) will encourage our honesty to surface and our healing to move forward?*

MATERIALS NEEDED: wedding candle, paper for writing, music, bowl, water, cloth.

GATHERING   All gather around the family table where Bill often fell asleep. His children also insist that his recliner, where he watched his beloved sports programs on TV and often slept in the months before he died, be brought close to the table. Gloria, his wife, lights their wedding candle in silence and asks her children to write on the paper in front of them the biggest hurt they need to let go of from their father. Each then folds the paper twice so that no one can see what is written on it.

STORYTELLING   *Oldest child:* We know that dad, like all dads, did his best. I'm especially grateful that he always (example of something good, e.g. came to my soccer games, even when I didn't play a lot and encouraged me to do well).

He then takes his folded paper and lights it from the wedding candle and puts it in a bowl in the middle of the table.

Second child: I'm grateful that dad always said he was sorry when (e.g. he got loud or missed some family event because he fell asleep). I always knew that he was trying to love us.

Burns slip and places it in bowl.

Third child (if necessary): I loved dad because he always praised me when (e.g. I got dressed for a dance or a date and told me I was the best child a father could want).

Burns paper and puts it in bowl.

Listen to how the psalmist calls upon God for help (Ps 25:6–7, 17–18):

> Remember your compassion and love, O Lord; for they are ages old. Remember no more the sins of my youth; remember me only in light of your love. Relieve the troubles of my heart; bring me out of my distress. Put an end to my affliction and suffering; take away all my sins.

Comments on it if possible. Otherwise there is silence.

Father's favorite song is played followed by spontaneous prayer.

Leader:

I want to pray for dad's peace and healing for us.
I want to pray for mom who always tried to help us see our goodness even when dad was rough to be with.
I want to pray for all children who feel hurt by their parents and think badly of themselves because of it.
I want to pray for all of us that we can take the good dad did and let go of the pain.

GESTURING Each then signs another member of the family with ashes from the bowl and in turn washes the ashes off.

SENDING An easy meal of pizza or soup follows. Whenever possible continue to tell stories of family hope and fun.

REFLECTION What have I done to let go of the painful events in our life? Who has helped most in doing this?

Admitting
Addiction

God, Grant me...
the serenity to accept the
things I cannot change,
the courage to change the
things I can and the wisdom
to know the difference.

ADDICTION TO ALCOHOL, DRUGS, FOOD, GAMBLING and so many other things has infected American society in ways even experts cannot assess. Almost every family has been hurt by addiction of some kind. Admitting addiction, therefore, and seeking treatment can be a tremendously relieving time for the families and friends of an addicted person.

Ralph had been drinking since he was thirteen years old. His parents usually took a glass of wine with dinner and Ralph was invited to do the same at a very early age. By the time he was eighteen, he had been drunk several times at high school parties. His family, though concerned, chalked it up to the stress of being a teenager.

Married at twenty-three, Ralph began to experience problems at work because of his weekend drinking. He often complained of headaches on Mondays and his supervisors noted his moodiness. His wife Betty wasn't sure what to do or say. Though a good husband and loving father, when he was drinking Ralph was given to outbursts of anger and rage. She was afraid.

Ralph admits now that he doesn't really remember his first child's baptism since he was so drunk. He began to miss work because of his drinking. His supervisor warned him about probation and called his wife. Betty started crying on the phone. Ralph's supervisor referred her to the substance abuse counselor where Ralph worked.

Betty went to see the counselor and together they decided to talk with Ralph. Within minutes of beginning their conversation, Ralph broke down and asked for help. He admitted his drinking was out of control but didn't know what to do about it. The counselor offered to accompany Ralph to an Alcoholics Anonymous meeting that afternoon. After ninety days of sobriety, Betty planned the following ritual.

INTENTION   Without denying her fears and concerns, Betty wanted to acknowledge her relief and pride in Ralph's early recovery. She also did not want to keep secrets from her children or closest friends.

In preparation for her celebration or yours we ask:

▸ *How do we affirm progress in life without dropping healthy boundaries?*
▸ *What gestures best express our unconditional love without denying our need for sanity?*

MATERIALS NEEDED: non-alcoholic beverage, empty beer or liquor bottle, the serenity prayer.

GATHERING   Betty invited Ralph's A.A. sponsor, his wife and two couples to whom they had grown very close. She asked each person to bring a favorite non-alcoholic drink. When everyone arrived, Betty asked everyone to gather in her family room where Ralph had often fallen into an alcoholic sleep. The television, which was usually on when Ralph drank, was playing without sound. Betty had a table set up with an empty beer bottle in the middle of it.

STORYTELLING   *Wife:* For a long time I did not help ____(name)____ by my denial. I always made excuses for him and his drinking to everyone. I'm really sorry that my shame made it too difficult for me to tell the truth.

A.A. sponsor: ____(Name)____, we're happy that you have been sober for ninety days. You are more peaceful and so are we. We're here today to thank you for your honesty and God for the help we received.

St. Luke reminds us that Jesus always forgives us (Lk 19:1–10):

> Jesus came to Jericho and intended to pass through the town. Now a man there named Zacchaeus, who was a chief tax collector and also a wealthy man, was seeking to see who Jesus was; but he could not see him because of the crowd, for he was short in stature. So he ran ahead and climbed a sycamore tree in order to see Jesus, who was about to pass that way. When he reached the place, Jesus looked up and said to him, "Zacchaeus, come down quickly, for today I must stay at your house." And he came down quickly and received him with joy. When they all saw this, they began to grumble, saying, "He has gone to stay at the house of a sinner." But Zacchaeus stood there and said to the Lord, "Behold, half of my possessions, Lord, I

shall give to the poor, and if I have extorted anything from anyone I shall repay it four times over." And Jesus said to him, "Today salvation has come to this house because this man too is a descendant of Abraham. For the Son of Man has come to seek and to save what was lost."

Comments on the friend's courage in recognizing his need and asking for help.

Recovering person: I tried to deny my addiction for a long time. Today I'm glad the Lord has asked me to eat with him again. Thank you for coming. I hope to live a sober life a day at a time.

GESTURING   All present speak about the non-alcoholic drink they brought and why they like it. Then each person offers a toast to healthy living. After all have shared, everyone takes the empty beer or liquor bottle to the trash and replaces it with a banner or poster of the serenity prayer:

> God grant me the serenity to accept the things I cannot change, courage to change the things I can and the wisdom to know the difference.

SENDING   All join hands in silence and pray that everyone can live a day at a time in sobriety and peace. All exchange hugs and move to the kitchen for a simple meal.

REFLECTION   If appropriate, all share answers to the question: What was the hardest thing I ever gave up?

PARISH   Parishes would do all a great service if they had regular services for those affected by addiction. To protect anonymity everyone in the parish could be invited to pray for addicts and families of addicts.

Losing a Job

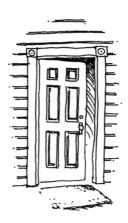

AMY HAD WORKED AS A WAITRESS to pay her way through college. After graduation, she took a two week vacation and began her career in the aerospace industry. She wanted to work even after marriage and arranged with her employers to work at home for six months after the birth of each of her children. When her employer lost most of its contracts with the government, Amy found herself out of a job for the first time in her adult life. She was devastated. After several months of fruitless and frantic searching for work, Amy knew she needed her friends more than ever. She created the following ritual.

INTENTION Amy was determined to find work. In the meantime, she wanted to gather with friends to accept the loss of her job and pray that she would be patient with herself and her family.

In preparation for her celebration or yours we ask:

▸ *How do we learn to accept loss especially when it is not our fault?*
▸ *What gestures might best express our loss and need for others at times like this?*

MATERIALS NEEDED: symbol of loss, symbol of hope, scented oil.

GATHERING Amy invited her closest friends from work, and her widowed mother who had always been her strength along with her husband and children. She asked the adults to bring some symbol of loss in their lives and a sign of hope.

STORYTELLING *Person out of work:* It is hard for me to look at you right now. I love you all very much but my work has always been a source of strength for me and I miss not having the security of a job.

Husband or friend: We all love you just the way you are. You are a good friend to us. We won't abandon you.

Listen to how Mark's gospel reminds us that God can do anything (Mk 10:23–27):

> Jesus looked around and said to his disciples, "How hard it is for those who have wealth to enter the kingdom of God!" The disciples were amazed at his words. So Jesus again said to them in reply, "Children, how hard it is to enter the kingdom of God! It is easier for a camel to pass through [the] eye of [a] needle than for one who is rich to enter the kingdom of God." They were exceedingly astonished and said among themselves, "Then who can be saved?" Jesus looked at them and said, "For human beings it is impossible, but not for God. All things are possible for God."

Offer comments on the passage if possible. For example: All of us have possessions we do not want to relinquish. For you it was your work. We are praying with you tonight that you will be able to let go, and trust God and us.

GESTURING   Each person holds up the item he or she brought to express loss and explains it—e.g. a picture of a parent lost to death; a high school yearbook that lacks someone's picture because he or she never graduated.

Whatever each brings is put outside the room. As each person returns to the room, he or she holds hands with the one who went before, until the person out of work, who is last, puts a symbol of her work outside the room and returns to complete the circle of people holding hands.

She then rubs oil on the hand of the person next to her, saying:

"May you walk in strength and courage with hope and trust."

Each person then anoints the person next to him or her in the same way.

SENDING   All pray the Our Father or some prayer all know.

REFLECTION   Share some event or story that helped you get on with your life again after a great loss.

Addressing the Pain of Special Family Days

LIKE SO MANY OTHERS with painful family problems, Maria dreaded the thought of special family gatherings. Inevitably, as these special days of celebration neared, she found herself remembering past hurts and wondering whether a new round of cutting and hurtful conversations was about to begin. Although she often spoke to her husband about her fears, he insisted that family celebrations were important for their children despite the sometimes heated atmosphere that developed when they gathered. So concerned was Maria with the thought of another spoiled family gathering that she even called a talk radio show looking for advice.

Maria's fears live quietly in most of us. Whether because of alcohol, drugs or other forms of abuse, many families have experienced the violent disruption of a family gathering causing them not to want to come together at all. There are many ways to address this problem. Below we offer two simple family rituals. The first is done at home even before going to the larger group. The second suggests ways for an extended family to pray honestly, gently and richly around their sometimes broken table.

INTENTION Maria needs to find a way to express her discomfort about family gatherings while honoring her husband's insistence about their importance. She wants her children to be able to express their feelings while enjoying the celebrations.

To celebrate their ritual or yours we ask:

▶ *How do we help children express feelings without lingering bitterness?*
▶ *What gesture will help the family name and heal their unresolved feelings?*

MATERIALS NEEDED: family candle, candle for each person.

GATHERING   Choose a time when everyone in the family is able to gather for at least fifteen minutes. After all have assembled, the leader lights the family candle in gratitude for the opportunity to gather. Then he or she invites each person present to light a candle from the first. In silence all hold hands for ten or fifteen seconds. The leader begins:

STORYTELLING   *Leader:* Thanksgiving (Christmas, Easter) is very near. It is a time of great joy for our family. At the same time, this celebration often brings a lot of tension to our lives. The light and happiness of being together with our extended family goes out. Take a moment to reflect on what is most difficult for you when we gather as an extended family. Then, after silently naming the person or situation that hurts or frightens you, extinguish your candle. (Wait for all to put candle out.)

Leader: Does anyone want to mention what hurts when we gather?

Give enough time for all to speak, but make sure everyone realizes that each one is not required to speak. Then someone reads.

Listen to the letter of James (3:10–18):

> From the same mouth come blessing and cursing. This need not be so . . . Does a spring gush forth from the same opening both pure and brackish water? Can a fig tree . . . produce olives, or a grapevine figs? Neither can salt water yield fresh.

GESTURING   *Leader:* Thank God our family is not just afflicted with tension and upset. Let's also share what we enjoy most when we gather. Let's speak about how we can be a light to others. After you share, please light a candle in gratitude.

Leader: (after all candles are lit) Repeat after me: Christ is our light! (three times)

All: Christ is our light! (three times)

SENDING   *Leader:* Every time you see a candle during these days of celebration, remember that you are not alone. All of us live in God and God is with us.

REFLECTION What is your best memory of a family gathering? How can you help make this next gathering one of our best?

Gathering of Families

MATERIALS NEEDED: symbolic gifts, a family quilt, blanket, tree or poster.

Before gathering, each family represented is asked to think of a symbol that best represents their gifts to the larger family. For example, an apron might symbolize the family that loves to bring food; a drawing of a door might represent the family that welcomes the larger family to their home for big celebrations.

STORYTELLING *Leader I:* Gathering can be difficult for many families. Because we come from such different backgrounds, it is easy to forget that all of us have different needs.

Leader II: Today let us take a moment to focus on our differences and be grateful for our diversity.

The Acts of the Apostles reminds us how to live (2:42–47):

> They devoted themselves to the teaching of the apostles and to the communal life, to the breaking of the bread and to the prayers. Awe came upon everyone, and many wonders and signs were done through the apostles. All who believed were together and had all things in common; they would sell their property and possessions and divide them among all according to each one's need. Every day they devoted themselves to meeting together in the temple area and to breaking bread in their homes. They ate their meals with exultation and sincerity of heart, praising God and enjoying favor with all the people. And every day the Lord added to their number those who were being saved.

Leader: In silence we pause to ask God for the courage to let go of a resentment, hurt or fear that lives inside us. (pause)

GESTURING | *Leader:* Having asked God for the faith to let go, may I ask a member of each family to bring their symbol forward and put it on our family quilt (tree, blanket, poster, etc.). As you do so, please tell the rest of us how your family treasure is a gift to the rest of us.

SENDING | *Leader:* Please respond: We thank you, O loving God, after each prayer.

That our earth might be treasured for all the gifts it offers us of food, clean water and shelter.

All: We thank you, O loving God.

Leader: That our families, especially those who cannot be present today, might grow in faith, harmony and peace.

All: We thank you, O loving God.

Leader: That God might heal our divisions and help us be a light in a very dark world.

All: We thank you, O loving God.

REFLECTION | If you could create a symbol of your choosing to represent your extended family, what would it be and why?

THROUGHOUT THE YEAR

The LITURGICAL CALENDAR is another wonderful way for us to pay attention to life and creation cycles in our faith lives. Advent, Christmas, Lent, Easter and Pentecost all invite us to celebrate our faith family's sacred story in union with Christians from around the world.

Many people already create and light an Advent wreath at home. In a society sometimes gone mad with consumerism, this simple ritual helps families remain focused on remembering that the simplicity of our Savior's birth challenges us to live modest lives. While not demeaning the sharing of gifts, rituals like the Advent wreath aid many families in limiting gift-giving.

Our own families use the ritual of Kris Kringle. Some time before Advent all of the adults take a name of another adult from a hat. That person is your Kris Kringle. He or she is the only person for whom you purchase a Christmas gift. We also commit ourselves to pray each day for the person whose name we have selected. All of the adults in our family agree that searching for presents for only one person makes gift-giving fun again at Christmas.

Lent, Easter and Pentecost also challenge us to remember and retell our central faith stories. Easter, which always arrives near the beginning of the spring, is a time to share our own resurrection stories. Who has been refreshing waters in your life this year? Who has helped you taste the joy of living? Taking a moment at Easter dinner to remember those people and events that have been so life-giving helps us appreciate the meaning of Jesus' suffering, death and resurrection. What a joy it must have been for the apostles to hear him say: Shalom, peace. Do not be afraid. I am with you.

Pentecost is Gaynell's favorite feast and season. She has always had an affection for the Holy Spirit. Because the sisters who taught her as a young woman loved the Holy Spirit, Gaynell found herself drawn to the numinous mystery of how God continues to dwell with us. She invites her family to place a message of peace in word or symbol on a Pentecost banner which all take outside to hang. Then her family and friends pray that the Spirit will take their prayers to the ends of the earth as healing breezes for all people and creation.

The seasons and feasts of the liturgical year hold a host of powerful memories and stories just begging to be celebrated in our homes. Learning about them can change the way we experience God and one another. They can also help us grow in our commitment to be good news for all the earth.

Celebrating Seasons

BRYAN CAME HOME EXCITED to tell everyone what he had learned in school about equinoxes and solstices. He had never before heard of them and was proud not only to be able to pronounce the words but also to explain them to his family. Enthusiastically, he told everyone they marked the entrance into each new season of the year and asked if his family could pay more attention to them. He suggested they mark the days on the calendar so everyone could celebrate. Smiling playfully, his older sister told Bryan that equinoxes and solstices were already on the calendar. He only had to look. Then she walked away.

Bryan's mom noticed his hurt. She put her arm around his shoulders and told him about how his grandfather welcomed each new season. On the first day of spring, grandpa would take all his children fishing and on the first day of summer he would light a bonfire. At the autumn equinox he would balance an egg and then bake a loaf of bread with it. Finally he would light candles for the winter equinox.

Bryan grew more and more excited as he listened to his mother. When she finished he asked her whether their family could do something special to mark the change of seasons. She readily agreed. Surprisingly so did everyone else in the family.

INTENTION The Williams family wanted to help all family members to try to identify how they experienced God in each season of the year. Their full ritual took one year to complete.

In preparation for their celebration or yours we ask (these questions should be asked before each seasonal celebration):

▸ *How do you experience the different seasons physically?*
▸ *How does the season reflect where you and your family are emotionally and spiritually right now?*

MATERIALS NEEDED: chosen poem, story, drawing or song, bells, bread (for fall), mistletoe (for winter), water, seeds, pot of soil (for spring), fire (for summer).

GATHERING   The family and a few friends gather in whatever room is most comfortable and affords the best outside view. All have been asked to bring a poem, song, story or saying that best expresses how they experience the season. The youngest children ring bells to start the celebration and welcome the season. The church often speaks of church bells opening space for prayer, scattering darkness and announcing God's presence.

STORYTELLING   Everyone is invited to share his or her story, song, poem or saying. Younger children can share a drawing. Then a scripture passage is read.

Fall   Read (Ps 67:7):

The earth has yielded its harvest; God, our God, blesses us.

Winter   Read (1 Thess 5:5–8):

For all of you are children of the light and children of the day. We are not of the night or of darkness. Therefore, let us not sleep as the rest do, but let us stay alert and sober . . . Since we are of the day, let us be sober, putting on the breastplate of faith and love and the helmet that is hope for salvation.

Spring   Read (Rev 22:1–2):

Then the angel showed me the river of life-giving water, sparkling like crystal, flowing from the throne of God and of the Lamb down the middle of its street. On either side of the river grew the tree of life that produces fruit twelve times a year, once each month; the leaves of the trees serve as medicine for the nations.

Summer   Read (Ps 74:16):

Yours the day and yours the night; you set the moon and sun in place.

GESTURING

Fall   *Leader:* There is a universal need to give thanks to God for the fruits of the earth. On this autumn equinox we ask God to fill us with thanks for all we have received. (Share one gift.)

Bread is broken and passed among all.

Winter   *Leader:* Mistletoe remains green all winter. It is a sign of strength, friendship and life. As we bundle mistletoe and tie it together with ribbon (do this), we share a part of ourselves that needs forgiveness in order to be "bundled" back together with family and friends.

Spring   All plant a seed in a large pot of soil and share that part of themselves they are planting for new growth. As the seeds are watered, all share how they will nourish themselves during the new season.

Leader: Water, as scripture reminds us, is a sign of new life. "A stream of life waters the earth and gives drink to the people." We are grateful for all of the people in our family who have been like refreshing waters to us.

Summer   Just before sunset, a fire is built to recall the psalmist's words that God will make a home in the sky for the sun which will warm the earth and make things grow.

Leader: On this summer solstice as we celebrate the longest day of the year, we take time to pray in thanksgiving for the way we have grown in faith.

Each shares an area of growth in life. Then all bow to the setting sun or the fire which represents it and pray in gratitude for all the gifts of creation.

SENDING   All offer a kiss of peace with the words: May God's peace clothe you during this season.

REFLECTION   Share your favorite activity of the season being celebrated.

PARISH   To enhance our appreciation for all creation, liturgy committees might suggest that banners be carried in procession and hung in church on the first Sunday of each new season. Before the closing blessing, a family could read a prayer commemorating the beginning of a new season.

Advent

ADVENT IS A SHORT SEASON of four weeks where days grow shorter and colder, nights longer and darker, and everyone begins to yearn for the return of the sun's warmth and light.

It is a waiting and preparing time. For Lennie, this was not easy. He remembered waiting for his sister to be born, for his birthday to come, for school to end and vacation to begin. In all of these waitings, he felt impatient, anxious and fretful. Waiting for a good thing to happen, like Christmas, seemed to take such a long time. He wished it were here.

Lennie's mother, aware of how anxious her son was, had many questions. How do we find the patience to stay where we are and not run away to something happening in another place or in the future? How do we enter the present moment and pay attention, be alert, stay awake and listen? What do we have to let go of to listen? What do we have to let go of to hear?

Together Lennie and his mom bought the ingredients to make a wreath. They would call it the "waiting wreath." Crafted in a circle, they placed greens and four candles on it. The circle reminded them that God was, is and always will be in their life. The pungent smells of the greens stirred their imagination for growth. The lighting of the candles, one for each week, warmed and gave light to their waiting. They also placed a "waiting cup" in the center of the wreath.

INTENTION   Lennie and his family wanted to create a space where they could wait together as a family, to affirm that there was something worth waiting for, and to listen to what was happening in their life right now. Once a week they celebrated the entire ritual. On the other days, in silence, they lit a candle for each week. Then they waited while people reflected on how they had tried to live their day fully. Straw was also available for anyone to place in the manger during Advent.

In preparation for their celebration or yours we ask:

▸ *What do you have to let go of to live in the present?*
▸ *How do you wait?*

MATERIALS NEEDED: four candles, wreath, cup, manger, straw, gong.

GATHERING   A gong sounds and a candle is lit.

Child: May this flame help us to see and hear what is happening within us now.

1st Week of Advent: PAY ATTENTION candle
2nd Week of Advent: BE ALERT candle
3rd Week of Advent: STAY AWAKE candle
4th Week of Advent: LISTEN candle

STORYTELLING   For each week someone tells a different story in response to the name of the candle.

1st week   A way you were able to PAY ATTENTION today was . . .

2nd week   A way you were able to BE ALERT today was . . .

3rd week   A way you were able to STAY AWAKE today was . . .

4th week   A way you were able to LISTEN today was . . .

Then someone reads.

Listen to Mark's advice (13:33–37):

> Be watchful! Be alert! You do not know when the time will come. It is like a man traveling abroad. He leaves home and places his servants in charge, each with his work, and orders the gatekeeper to be on the watch. Watch, therefore; you do not know when the lord of the house is coming, whether in the evening, or at midnight, or at cockcrow, or in the morning. May he not come suddenly and find you sleeping. What I say to you, I say to all: "Watch!"

GESTURING   *Leader:* The waiting cup is a sign we are one family as we prepare for Christmas by living the present moment fully. It mingles our lives together as we wait. We pass it in silence. As you drink, think of how we can be life and hope for one another.

SENDING   Gong sounds.

Leader: Let us extinguish our candle(s) as we welcome the darkness of waiting.

As people leave or begin their meal, straw is placed in the manger. Each piece represents the action of living and responding to the present happenings of their day. Throughout the Advent season, anyone can place straw in the manger. Some of this straw is later brought to the crèche scene at the parish church.

REFLECTION   Tell a story of waiting that really changed you.

PARISH   After communion on the last Sunday of Advent, parishes might invite children to place straw from their home manger in the parish manger. This custom might also help children who have not celebrated first eucharist feel more a part of the worshiping assembly.

Thanksgiving

THANKSGIVING IS A FAMILY DAY, a time to gather with relatives and remember the blessings God has given us. The Evans family always had a large gathering at their home. All the guests brought their favorite traditional Thanksgiving dish. The Sullivans prepared candied sweet potatoes. The Gallaghers baked chocolate pie, using the same recipe their great-grandparents used. Grandma's oyster dressing complemented Louise's merliton casserole and Uncle Albert's artichoke/spinach dish. The Evanses only had to roast the turkey, prepare a homemade cranberry sauce and set the table. Actually, there were a series of tables stretching through the living room. They were covered with the same orange tablecloths that had been used for the last ten years. Grandma offered to make new ones but the children protested. The orange tablecloths had too many memories.

The Evanses had a special day in every season: Christmas in winter, Easter in spring, Pentecost in summer, Thanksgiving in autumn. Thanksgiving was a time they gathered both people and the harvest to praise God for all the gifts of creation.

INTENTION The Evans family wanted to gather friends and relatives to share a meal of thanks and to name the blessings in their lives. Conscious of an uncle and a great-grandmother who had died during the past year, they wanted their names included in the ritual lighting of the candles.

In preparation for their ritual or yours we ask:

▶ *What has happened in our family during the past year?*
▶ *Are there new people to invite?*
▶ *What gesture will best express our acceptance of the growing diversity in our family?*

MATERIALS NEEDED: four candles representing north, south, east and west, bells, a cup filled with wine or juice, a candle for each family in front of each mother's place at table and an extra candle for families everywhere.

GATHERING   The children ring bells as people come to the table.

Leader: To all places the call goes out to gather the harvest of the earth and the people of the harvest (bells ring). Called from the four directions, we gather that all may be one. We gather from the north (bells ring, candle is lit); we gather from the east (bells rings, candle is lit); we gather from the south (bells ring, candle is lit); we gather from the west (bells ring, candle is lit). And we say welcome to this dwelling place of the Lord. We are a sacred people, for the Lord dwells within and among us as family.

In this circle of life, we light our family candles.

(Each mother lights her family candle, saying:) I light this candle for my family ____(names people in her family living and dead)____. Every day I give thanks for their presence in my life.

Leader: We light this candle for families everywhere. We give thanks for our oneness as the family of God. In the silence of our hearts we give thanks for the many gifts that are ours (pause).

Let us be mindful of those who are without food or shelter (pause).

And let us remember those whom we love who are not now present at our table. Please mention anyone not here you want us to remember.

STORYTELLING   People join hands and offer thanks or speak of their needs. (During the meal, the stories behind these prayers can be shared.)

GESTURING   The blessing cup is passed in silence. Everyone tastes of the goodness of God in the lives of one another.

SENDING   *Leader:* We believe that all creation prays and gives thanks to God by being totally who they are. We breathe in love from this circle of life. As we breathe out, we send this love to all people. (Pause. Then bells are rung as everyone says:)

SO BE IT. SO BE IT. SO BE IT.

Christmas

DECORATING THE HOUSE, BUYING GIFTS, sending packages to relatives, baking cookies, preparing food, not to mention the children's excitement as they anticipated Christmas, had made Monica weary. Would she be able to finish everything? As she sat and reflected, she realized that this had been happening every year—and not only to her but to other members of the family as well.

What was the meaning of Christmas anyway? Yes, it was a time of gift-giving but wasn't it also a celebration of what we have been given, of what we have received? Monica believed deeply that all of life was a gift from God. But how does one remember and live that daily? How might she help her family see they were gifts to one another?

She smiled as she thought of Tony who seemed so unable to speak of what was troubling him. He was like a tightly wrapped gift, difficult to open. Then she laughed when she thought of others, loosely wrapped and willing to speak of everything in life! Thinking about her family made Monica remember the short Rossetti poem she had learned in high school:

> What shall I give him, poor as I am?
> If I were a shepherd, I would give him a lamb.
> If I were a wise man I would do my part.
> What shall I give him? Give him your heart.

But what was her heart? And what was the heart of her family right now? How does one receive this gift of God in Jesus? Finally, she shared her feelings with her family. She was surprised that their sentiments were so close to hers. Together they planned the following ritual for Christmas eve. Before her family gathered, everyone picked a name of another person in the family and chose an object which best symbolized that person.

INTENTION   Monica and her family wanted to affirm each other as gift and offer a way for each member to grow in self-worth.

In preparation for their celebration or yours, we ask:

▸ *How do you see and appreciate others as gift?*
▸ *How do you receive and accept yourself as gift to others?*
▸ *How do you recognize the gift you are from God?*

MATERIALS NEEDED: objects that symbolize each person in the family, yule candle, decorated Advent wreath, cookies.

GATHERING	A yule candle burns in the middle of an Advent wreath. Her French heritage taught her a custom of decorating the candle with ribbons and greenery on the eve of Christ's coming as light. Then the family symbols were placed on the tablecloth they would use for their Christmas meal.
STORYTELLING	*Leader:* On the birth of Jesus as light in our life, may we see more clearly the gift of who we are and the gift of who Jesus is. May this light of Christ be kindled in our hearts.

All present take a turn and hold their item which symbolizes the person they chose and explain why they selected it.

For example: I have chosen glasses for you, Hank, because you seem to be aware of what is happening not only in the world but here in our family. You notice small things and take the time to speak of them.

Younger son: I have chosen sneakers for you, Elizabeth. Your feet have taken you to places and people where I am afraid to go. You began a new job and still found time to come and see my soccer games.

After all share, someone reads:

Let us listen to John's gospel when he speaks of Jesus as Word made flesh and light (Jn 1:1–5, 14–15):

> In the beginning was the Word, and the Word was with God, and the Word was God. He was in the beginning with God. All things came to be through him, and without him nothing came to be. What came to be through him was life, and this life was the light of the human race; the light shines in the darkness, and the darkness has not overcome it . . . And the Word became flesh and made his dwelling among us, and we saw his glory, the glory as of the Father's only Son, full of grace and truth.

GESTURING   All respond by accepting the object symbolizing them and mentioning something they like about themselves. Like a light shining in the darkness, they now plan how to give it away.

Sing Christmas carols, tell Christmas stories, roast chestnuts and eat Christmas cookies.

SENDING   All warm their hands over the Yule flame and offer a sign of appreciation to each person in the family.

REFLECTION   What is your fondest Christmas memory?

Ashes from Ashes

THE RAMIREZ FAMILY WAS GROWING UP. Two generations old in the United States, they had maintained their Mexican and Catholic identity but were searching for ways to grow more deeply in faith. The home rituals they had learned from their grandparents had always been important to them. So too were the rituals they celebrated in their parish churches. One Shrove Tuesday they decided to end Mardi Gras and begin Lent in their own home, then go to their parish church to complete the ritual on Ash Wednesday. Committed to economic justice for all, especially Mexican Americans, they wanted to express their dreams and hopes in a faith-filled way. They designed the following ritual for use at their home table and with their parish family.

INTENTION The Ramirez family, committed to deepening their bonds as family and contributing to the parish community as well, want to begin Lent with a powerful reminder that together they can help their families and parishes grow and change.

In order to plan their celebration or yours, we ask:

▸ *How can we reinforce healthy family bonds?*
▸ *What action can we use to symbolically express our desire to grow in love for one another and our commitment to justice?*

MATERIALS NEEDED: pencils, paper, strong bowl, matches, instrumental music.

GATHERING	Grandparents, parents, children and grandchildren all gather at one family's home. If the gathering is not too large, it would also be wonderful to invite a family of new immigrants to the celebration.

STORYTELLING

Grandfather: Today we gather full of joy and accomplishment. We have supported one another as family and have grown in our faith and commitment to justice. (He speaks spontaneously about some good work of his family, e.g. working to help resettle families or find jobs for new immigrants.)

Grandmother: We gather on Sundays, praise God, eat together, support our children, especially in faith, and remember that together we can accomplish so much. (Shares a special story about how her own parents or grandparents gathered—e.g. Mardi Gras in Mexico.)

Father: Tonight we gather in gratitude for who we are and what we have become. More importantly, we want to take a few moments to think quietly about how this Lent might be a time of personal and family growth. (Silence)

St. Paul's letter helps us understand Lent more deeply. Listen (Phil 4:4–7):

> Rejoice in the Lord always. I shall say it again: rejoice! Your kindness should be known to all. The Lord is near. Have no anxiety at all, but in everything, by prayer and petition, with thanksgiving, make your requests known to God. Then the peace of God that surpasses all understanding will guard your hearts and minds in Christ Jesus.

GESTURING

Mother: Tonight you will find a piece of paper near your place at the table. Simply write one fault you would like to rid yourself of and one virtue you want to build up. Fold the paper and pass it to the person on your right to hold. That person will pray for your strength.

After all have completed this task:

Eldest child: Please place the paper you are holding in the bowl in the middle of the table. (He or she then lights a match and burns the papers. All sit in silence.)

Second child: Turns on quiet instrumental music, picks up the bowl of ashes (after checking that it has cooled), turns to the person on his or her left and says while putting ashes on the hand:

May you grow in hope this Lent.

The person signed takes the bowl and signs the next person in the same way.

Third child (if appropriate): Tomorrow I will take these ashes, symbolic of our families' commitment to grow in faith, to our parish church. There they will be mixed with the ashes of other families and our parish family. In this way all who come for ashes will be signed in our commitment and we in theirs. We also send these blessed and mingled ashes to the homebound.

SENDING   All join hands and pray the Our Father (in the language proper to your family). Next, extend hands over one another and bless your family with these words:

May Lent lead us to Easter and the hope of everlasting life.

REFLECTION   What most impressed you about your family's shared faith?
Have you ever felt the strength of your faith? Describe.
What are your hopes for your parish?

PARISH   At the principal celebration of Ash Wednesday, families who have celebrated an "ashes" ritual at home process with their home ashes and mix them with the ashes of the parish. The celebrant might say something like: "Letting go of our faults, sins and unhealthy patterns of living can be very difficult. Together, symbolized by these mingled ashes, we walk through Lent toward Easter knowing we are not alone."

Easter

ARTH SOFTENS, FLOWERS BUD, WATER FLOWS, and sun warms a
spring season of new hope. It is Easter! Jamie always felt a newness
on the feast of the Resurrection. She had memories of new clothes, a straw
hat and white gloves. She remembered scattering the dew which covered
her shoes as she hunted for Easter eggs.

Her Aunt Mary had taught her how to braid and bake Easter bread.
And she treasured the shawl each person wore for storytelling which was
given to her by her grandmother. Her son Robie called it the Talking Shawl,
like the Talking Feather of the native peoples of the north. Whoever holds
the feather tells stories while the group listens. How like the early church
where people gathered for the Easter vigil, lit a candle, told stories, blessed
water and renewed promises.

Jamie's family had been very busy this past year. It seemed they were
becoming workaholics. Sunday was no longer a day of rest—a time set
aside, different than the other days of the week. And rest—well, they really
didn't know how to slow down as a family.

INTENTION Jamie and her family wanted to celebrate the new life promised by the
resurrection. They also hoped to find a way to make every Sunday of the
year a sabbath, a day of rest.

In preparation for their celebration or yours we ask:

▶ *What are the signs and stories of hope—personal and scriptural—which speak honestly of who
and where you are right now?*
▶ *How do you make Sunday a day of rest?*

MATERIALS NEEDED: musical instruments, bells, decorated candle, shawl,
Easter bread.

GATHERING | As family and friends gather, the children make a joyful noise with musical instruments, mainly bells. Their sound lifts the hearts of all gathered. Signs of hope are pasted or drawn on the candle. The candle is lit.

STORYTELLING | *Parent:* "Christ is the light of the world. May this light dispel the darkness of our hearts and minds."

Second parent: Puts the shawl on and tells a story.

For example: Jamie speaks of her grandmother knitting this shawl for her. "In every stitch I thought of you and loved you," her grandmother had told her. Whenever she wears this shawl she feels she is connected and loved. It brings new hope to her, like the white garment of baptism. She feels clothed by the family of God.

The shawl is passed and worn by each person who chooses to tell his or her own personal, family and/or scripture stories of hope. Finally, someone reads:

Listen to the Easter story from Matthew's gospel (28:5–6):

> Then the angel said to the women in reply, "Do not be afraid! I know that you are seeking Jesus the crucified. He is not here, for he has been raised just as he said. Come and see the place where he lay."

GESTURING | All present extend their hands to bless the Easter bread:

Leader: Bless this bread, O Lord.
May it be a sign of thanksgiving and hope.

As the bread is passed, each person breaks off a piece and holds it. When everyone has a piece, each person takes a moment to pray in silence for the person who gave it to him or her. All eat.

SENDING | Family games, rest and entertainment follow.

REFLECTION   What is your favorite memory of spring?

▸ *After this celebration, the family chose to break bread together on the Sabbath every week.*

PARISH   Parishes might invite families to bring bells for a Sunday celebration. The bells would be rung before the liturgy of the word, the telling of our family faith stories.

Pentecost

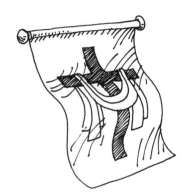

FEAR. SOMETIMES IT CAME QUICKLY and unexpectedly, immobilizing. Althea remembered mispronouncing the word "heir" in eighth grade. Everyone laughed. Even with the teacher's help she could not remember the sound when she had to read it aloud. Everyone laughed again. She could still feel her heart pounding, her clammy hands and the closed-in feeling. In almost every new situation, she felt the same way.

Now Althea's entire family seemed afflicted. Her daughter had just shared a similar experience anticipating her first interview for a teaching position. Her son Mark, who never seemed afraid to try out for a ball team, panicked taking tests. Her youngest son, Billy, a first grader, had difficulty beginning school. The whole first month he said he was afraid he would never make any friends.

As the time of Pentecost arrived, the image of God's life as fire, wind, and soaring dove filled her heart. In recent years she thought of the Holy Spirit as God's breath. This image assured her that, despite all her fears, she was never alone. Like the men and women behind locked doors two thousand years ago, she was filled with the breath of God. If they could leave those rooms to be peacemakers in the world, Althea and her family could do the same. She was anxious to celebrate Pentecost with her family.

INTENTION　In preparation for their celebration or yours we ask:

▶ *What is your memory of a past or present experience that filled you with fear? How did you handle it?*

▶ *What do you need to help you overcome or live with your fear as you reach out to others?*

▶ *What is the message of courage and peace you would send to the earth?*

MATERIALS NEEDED: four candles, cloth or paper for a prayer flag.

GATHERING   Family and friends gather outside and light a circle of four candles which represent the four directions. In doing so they acknowledge that we are one people in receiving the breath of God.

Using a breathing prayer, the group becomes quiet.

Leader: Imagine yourself inhaling God's breath of love and exhaling this holy breath to people you love.

STORYTELLING   Each family member shares an experience of fear in his or her life.

Then one of them reads:

Let us listen to the experience of Pentecost recorded in the Acts of the Apostles (2:1–8):

> When the time for Pentecost was fulfilled, they were all in one place together. And suddenly there came from the sky a noise like a strong driving wind, and it filled the entire house in which they were. Then there appeared to them tongues as of fire, which parted and came to rest on each one of them. And they were all filled with the Holy Spirit and began to speak in different tongues, as the Spirit enabled them to proclaim. Now there were devout Jews from every nation under heaven staying in Jerusalem. At this sound, they gathered in a large crowd, but they were confused because each one heard them speaking in his own language. They were astounded, and in amazement they asked, "Are not all these people who are speaking Galileans? Then how does each of us hear them in his own native language?"

GESTURING   Each family member draws a symbol or message of peace and healing for the world on the prayer flag. For example, Mark drew a cloud full of rain for all who need clean water.

After everyone has time to draw, all hold the flag or place it in a holder.

SENDING   In a circle around the prayer flag, all imagine the breath of God carrying their messages to the four directions. Turning to each of the directions they offer a blessing of fearlessness to the world. Then they offer this same blessing to one another.

REFLECTION   What is your biggest challenge as a peacemaker?

PARISH   Parishes might collect family prayer flags for display in church the Sunday after Pentecost. The families who made them would join the entrance procession carrying their flags. At the prayer of the faithful a member of each family could take their family flag to the front of the church and together with others wave them as all pray for world peace.

Bibliography

Bausch, William, *Storytelling: Imagination and Faith* (Mystic: Twenty-Third Publications, 1984).

Cooke, Bernard, *Sacraments and Sacramentality* (Mystic: Twenty-Third Publications, 1983).

Cronin, Gaynell Bordes, *Holy Days and Holidays* (Minneapolis: Winston Press, 1979).

———, *Holy Days and Holidays, II* (San Francisco: Harper, 1988).

———, *Activities for the Christian Family* (Mahwah: Paulist Press, 1980).

———, *Sunday Throughout the Week* (Notre Dame: Ave Maria Press, 1981).

Driver, Tom F., *The Magic of Ritual* (San Francisco: Harper, 1991).

A Family Perspective in Church and Society (Washington, D.C.: U.S. Catholic Conference, 1988).

Feinstein, David, and Peg Elliott Mayo, *Rituals for Living & Dying* (San Francisco: Harper, 1990).

Fischer, Kathleen, *The Inner Rainbow: The Imagination in Christian Faith Life* (Mahwah: Paulist Press, 1983).

Fulghum, Robert, *From Beginning to End: The Rituals of Our Lives* (New York: Villard Books, 1995).

Geffen, Rela M., ed., *Celebration and Renewal: Rites of Passage in Judaism* (Philadelphia: The Jewish Publication Society, 1993).

Harris, Maria, *Dance of the Spirit* (New York: Bantam Books, 1989).

Hays, Edward, *Prayers for the Domestic Church: A Handbook for Worship in the Home* (Easton, Kans.: Forest of Peace Books, 1979).

———, *Prayers for a Planetary Pilgrim* (Easton, Kans.: Forest of Peace Books, 1988).

Imber-Black, Evan, and Janine Roberts, *Rituals for Our Times* (New York: Harper Collins, 1987).

Lane, Belden C., *Landscapes of the Sacred* (Mahwah: Paulist Press, 1988).

Lee, Bernard, and Michael Corvan, *Dangerous Memories* (Kansas City, Mo.: Sheed and Ward, 1986).

Lieberman, Susan Abel, *New Traditions—Redefining Celebrations for Today's Families* (San Jose: Resource Publications, 1987).

Martos, Joseph, *Doors to the Sacred* (New York: Doubleday, 1982).

McKenna, Megan, *Parables* (Maryknoll: Orbis, 1994).

———, *Not Counting Women and Children* (Maryknoll: Orbis, 1994).

Nelson, Gertrud Muller, *To Dance with God—Family Ritual and Community Celebration* (Mahwah: Paulist Press, 1986).

Progoff, Ira, *At a Journal Workshop: The Basic Text and Guide for Using the Intensive Journal* (New York: Dialogue House Library, 1975).

Rathschmidt, John, and Gaynell Bordes Cronin, *Celebrating the Church Year with Children* (videos) (Mahwah: Paulist Press, 1994).

Roberto, John, *Family Rituals and Celebrations* (New Rochelle: Don Bosco Multimedia, 1992).

———, *Rituals for Sharing Faith* (New Rochelle: Don Bosco Multimedia, 1992).

Rupp, Joyce, *Praying Our Goodbyes* (Notre Dame: Ave Maria Press, 1988).

———, *May I Have This Dance* (Notre Dame: Ave Maria Press, 1992).

Shenk, Sara Wenger, *Why Not Celebrate* (Intercourse, Pa.: Good Books, 1987).

Simpkinson, Charles and Anne, *Sacred Stories: A Celebration of the Power of Story To Transform and Heal* (San Francisco: Harper, 1993).

Some, Malidoma Patrice, *Ritual: Power, Healing and Community* (Portland, Ore.: Swan/Raven & Company, 1979).

Thomas, David, *Family Life and the Church* (Mahwah: Paulist Press, 1979).

Viorst, J., *Necessary Losses* (New York: Fawcett Gold Medal, 1986).

Westerhoff, John H., and William Willimon, *Liturgy and Learning Through the Life Cycle* (New York: Seabury Press, 1980).

Wright, Wendy M., *Sacred Dwelling: A Spirituality of Family Life* (New York: Crossroad, 1990).